FUSE

Igniting the Full Power of the Creative Economy:
A 21st Century Primer for Boomers and Millennials in the Workplace

Jim Finkelstein

Mary Gavin

ISBN: 1-4392-1239-2
ISBN-13: 9781439212394
LCCN: 2008910949

Visit www.futuresense.com/FUSE to order additional copies.

FUSE

Terms of Endearment

Names for the Newest Generation of Workers

Millennials
Generation Y
iGeneration
Digital Natives
Generation Why
Generation Whiner
Generation 2.0
Generation Me
Gamers
ADHD Generation
Echo Boomers
Net Generation
Reagan Babies
Second Baby Boom
Boomer Babies
Generation XX
D.A.R.E. Generation
Google Generation
MySpace Generation
MyPod Generation
Generation Next
Nintendo Generation
Cynical Generation
Generation 9/11

Next (or Second)
  Greatest Generation
Generation C –
  for connected
Generation.com
Generation 2000
Generation Tech
Adultolescents
Generation O –
  for Obama

Acknowledgements and Dedication

No writer goes through the labor and delivery of a book manuscript without a lot of help: a cheering section, a keen editor, friends who bring meals, reviewers who drop their own work to read and comment on the latest chapter, family members with infinite patience for missed weekends, dinners, bedtimes and social and sports events. Our first vote of thanks goes to Margaret Walker and Matt Finkelstein, our FutureSense colleagues, for their research skills, good cheer, thoughtful discussion and always constructive commentary. We also thank Lynn, Brett, Kahala and Ernie; and Tim, Stevo and Sarei for their constant love, and their belief in our ideas.

This book is dedicated to all of the SENIOROOMER-GENXENNIALS™ among us. Those who have found the creative genius in all generations and a way to use it all in the workplace ... from the great-grandparents who are texting up a storm to the recent high school grads who have entered the workforce and need to make a basic living.

We honor those who are dedicated to transforming a 20th century workplace to be more relevant to the 21st century workforce ... those who recognize that we have moved beyond the industrial and technology and information ages to one of the most creative renaissances in our history... those who are willing to look beyond the traditional and known to the untried and unknown ... and finally, to those who will take the time to find an "aha" or two – the FUSIONS – in our book and apply them in their working lives.

– Jim Finkelstein and Mary Gavin

Table of Contents

The Starting Point

> "The last few decades have belonged to a certain kind of person with a certain kind of mind – computer programmers who could crank code, lawyers who could craft contracts, MBAs who could crunch numbers. But the keys to the kingdom are changing hands. The future belongs to a very different kind of person with a very different kind of mind – creators and empathizers, pattern recognizers, and meaning makers. These people ... will now reap society's richest rewards...." [1]

When Daniel Pink proclaimed the end of the Information Age in 2006, most of us in the Boomer Generation shrugged, slightly embarrassed that we hadn't caught that wave the first time through. Yes, we knew that technology was changing the world – we used the Internet ourselves for emails, real-time sports news and comparison shopping. Yes, our kids had their noses not to the grindstone, but to LCD displays. And yes, the young people our companies were hiring seemed bizarrely competent and confident, given their lack of maturity. But Boomers have long defined the world – of work, politics, relationships, consumerism, religion, art – in our own terms, by our own reflections.

If we didn't perceive it, it didn't exist.

Enter the Millennials – the iGeneration, Generation Y, Gamers, Digital Natives, whatever you want to call all

80 million Americans born roughly between 1975 and 1995 – who process information differently than the rest of us – conceptually, in parallel processes, looking not particularly for answers, but for options. It is a generation with unique skills: Weaned on video games, its members are competitive, competent, collaborative, passionate, persistent and self-possessed. It is a generation with a unique mindset based on its own almost **universal experience with technology**, *an experience not shared by any other generation.*

It is a generation that is changing the world of work.

This book decodes that generation for employers, and decodes the workplace for that generation. We use Millennials and Boomers as our bookends, both because their sheer numbers dominate the workplace, and because they fill the roles of peons and bosses at this point in time. Our goal is to show that a Millennial/Boomer *mashup* – not a gap – but a *fusion* of their unique and specific perspectives and abilities – will lead to innovation, and speed products, services and people into the creative economy of the future.

What's a mashup? Information and presentation separated and remixed to create novel forms of reuse. It's an organic form of innovation that's evolved because the democratization and speed of information of the World Wide Web has dissolved boundaries between disciplines. Our mashup is between 20th century work*places* and 21st century work*forces*, between the experience, command and linearity of Boomers and the technosmarts, consensus and boundaryless thought of Millennials, which is freeing innovation to evolve a novel future for every organization.

"Think outside the box? OK. There is no box...." [2]

Why does this require yet another management book?

Because Millennials are different from Boomers in work styles, risk taking, rewards and ROI. This translates to Millennials' collective inability to find a clear, satisfying career path; an 80% rate of job dissatisfaction; and a very high cost of turnover ($75k per).

Because organizations, managed largely by Boomers, must have Millennial workers as 64 million skilled Boomers will retire by the end of the decade.

Because the workplace itself – the environment and context of getting the job done – is being transformed by information technology, media 2.0, multi-level data streams, 24/7 business hours, brutal global competition and just plain speed – speed of thought, speed of action, speed of results.

And because today's workplace change is exponential, not the incremental change of the past. It is fast, it is furious, and it can be fatal to organizations that cannot understand how to leverage it to their advantage.

> Organizations need to create a mashup of the
> 20th century workplace and the 21st century
> workforce.

This book has been informed by many sources. Fifty years of collective management experience by the authors. Case studies of client problems. A nationwide survey detailing Millennials' workplace attitudes and aspirations. Substantive research into current workplace mores and modalities. A great deal of thoughtful concern and discourse with educators and change leaders about the students and workers of the present and the workplace of the future. And good old-fashioned common sense, tempered by a bit of nostalgia for the hierarchical workplaces of the past, and a great deal of eager anticipation for the organic, evolutionary workplaces of the present and future.

FUSE is really a blog between covers. It is the *Cliffs Notes* (Boomers) or *Spark Notes* (Millennials) version of the mashup between the 20th century workplace and the 21st century workforce. It presents information in accessible, bite-size chunks for those with even the shortest attention spans. It is opinionated, often irreverent, and offers a lot of the best current thought by others (with attribution, of course) entwined with our own. Each chapter ends with a FUSION text box, highlighting the irreducible key points from the chapter – an "aha!" or two that you can apply to your own workplace situations to leverage change.

There are five chapters for Employers (Boomers) and five for Millennials, which makes the book perfect for training purposes. The writing style, research and presentation used for the different generations are keyed to their different expectations. However, the chapters are not generationally proprietary. As one of our Millennial reviewers put it, *"One of our most interesting revelations upon reading FUSE is that it expanded our consciousness not just about the other generation, but also significantly about **ourselves**."*

Every point will not correspond to every Millennial, or to every Boomer. There is a great deal of personal individuation within the generations, there are regional and cultural differences, there are gender anomalies. Yet there are such strong trend lines within the groups that our topics are useful in both the general and in the particular. We chose the chapter subjects by virtue of the challenges they present in the workplace today, and those begging for understanding to create the workplaces of tomorrow. These culminate in the topic of innovation, and our deeply held belief that we haven't seen anything yet: Whatever your service or product line, the innovations that will be brought by a wholly leveraged, wired workforce are the energy that will fuel 21st century creativity, productivity and profitability.

For deeper investigation of our topics, we hope that you'll browse the Notes on Sources pages. We strongly recommend the seminal works on many of the topics covered in this book: those on generations in the workplace written by Strauss & Howe, on gamers by Beck & Wade, on mobilizing generation 2.0 by Ben Rigby, on generation me by Jean Twenge, and anything written by Marc Prensky, McCrindle Research, or Penelope Trunk in her Brazen Careerist dress. [3]

FUSE is not static. Please give us survey responses, FUSIONS and comments at www.futuresense.com/FUSE, most of all to answer the question: **What is the one new thing that you are thinking about because you read this book?** Many thanks.

For Employers

"Just like you, I've experienced the drama of the college kids who have their mothers negotiate their offers for them, the new MBA who tells the vice president that she won't travel unless she has 'at least two weeks' notice,' and the interns who refuse to stuff binders. The chilling fact, though, is that we ain't seen nothin' yet!" [4]

⌘　⌘　⌘

"By the year 2012, (Millennials) will have filled the 18-34 (workforce) age group." [5]

⌘　⌘　⌘

"The Millennials may well end up being the ideal workers: they possess the 'can do' commitment of the seniors, the teamwork ethic of the Boomers and the techno-savvy of the Xers." [6]

Chapter 1
Millennials: Slackers or Superheroes?

"This is the most high-maintenance workforce in the world. The good news is that they're also going to be the most high-performing." [7]

There is little debate over the attributes of Millennial workers, but furious disagreement over how to decode those attributes for the workplace.

Millennials are the 80 million Americans roughly between the ages of 15 and 30. [8] Over 50 million of them are old enough to be employees. They have grown up with electronic media as their primary source of learning, producing and, often, interacting. Every generation is different from the ones before it, because environment shapes individual and group behavior. But this generation is manifestly different, as it has been shaped not by understanding the natural world and manipulating its resources, but by artificial intelligence and virtual relationships.

There are more Millennials than Boomers. Their sheer numbers added to their unique norms are changing the social and business landscape. As is true of land armies, the larger the force, the more likely the victory. The Millennials will outlast and outlive the Boomers.

How are they so different from their predecessors, especially as employees?

They are individuals, of course, with unique character traits and novel sensibilities. Every distribution curve has a tail. Also, in the US, those on the coasts differ from those in the center and southern states in exposure to nonhierarchical institutions, in dress, and in expectations, among other attributes. However, Millennials are almost universally perceived as tech-savvy, project-oriented multitaskers; as competitive gamers who enjoy risk and court reward passionately. They are collaborative, color-blind, and socially conscious. Their choices focus on output, not method. They learn experientially, by trial and error. Philosophically speaking, they balance the material wonders of technology with the spiritual demands of our human nature. [9]

Again factoring individual exceptions, they are also widely perceived as largely self-centered, short-sighted, ignorant of cultural and social mores, and high-maintenance. They want instant gratification, from feedback to promotions. Their focus is on life balance. They question everything from a position of undifferentiated equality, and have supremely unrealistic expectations. Practically speaking, they are loud, pierced, entitled and unapologetic.

Their Boomer managers, who have shaped the workplace and the workforce in their own image, just don't understand what makes this generation tick.

That lack of understanding portends a very poor outcome for both groups.

- Younger employees report 600 percent more job dissatisfaction than older employees.
- 80% of Millennials dislike their jobs.
- The average Millennial will have 8.6 jobs between the ages of 18 and 32.
- At an average $75,000 worker replacement cost, not understanding the new generation of workers is an extremely expensive exercise in futility. [10]

So let's do a little decoding of this new generation.

The pros and cons of the Millennial generation are laid out in Got Game: How the Gamer Generation is Reshaping Business Forever; and in Generation Me.[11] Both detail the Millennial mentality. Each forms its own unique, and wildly disparate, conclusions.

Got Game claims gamers will rewrite American – actually global – business, based on unique gamer skills of risk-taking, reward-seeking and goal-scoring, traits that can be infinitely replayed until victory is achieved. Generation Me looks to fill in the territory between soaring expectations and crushing realities, detailing the Millennial's bouts of uncertainty, anxiety and depression, despite the highest levels of support, education and opportunity in history.

Both sets of conclusions are based on solid data: The Gamer book is based on 2,000 detailed survey responses taken by Millennial members in the last 5 years; the Me book is based on psychological survey data from 1.3 million young Americans over 4 decades.

In fact, Millennials are neither saints nor sinners, slackers nor superheroes.

They are a cohort of employees with unique skills and mindset who, if managed to potential, are absolutely capable of changing the way we do business for the better across the world.

> *"Reality changed much faster than our attitudes."* [12]

The first thing to do is to **understand them.** Not completely, but enough to share some perspective. Understand that Boomers love to tell tales of the Millennials' narcissism and entitlement, because it makes the Boomers look so good by comparison. But **Millennial attributes are neither right nor wrong**, even when measured against Boomer expectations: They are just different.

Consider the effect of video games on this generation, and the viewpoint that gaming makes this generation unique.

As detailed in <u>Got Game</u>, *"What gives digital games the power to transform practical life is that they have been adopted wholesale by people of one age group and largely ignored by everyone older than that."* Video games offer an alternative reality that has caused systematically different ways of working, systematically different skills to learn, and systematically different goals in life. Games are a $22 billion industry worldwide, with 4,000 titles produced a year. 92% of Millennials play them. Gamer values have infiltrated Millennial culture, and are now being brought into the workplace. [13]

To the Boomers reading this book: **Have you EVER played a video game?** Take a small personal risk and just do it. It doesn't matter if you play with a Wii or Xbox 360 or PlayStation3 or an iPhone. You can rent a game console and games at major video outlets such as Blockbuster, or you can go to an electronics store and leverage the experience of the staff. They'll fix you up with the virtual reality equivalent of a blind date. Just as in the real world, it will be an eye-opening experience.

Besides gamer mentality, **entitlement**, often confused with instant gratification, is another Millennial trait that drives Boomer managers crazy.

Is it real? Yes. Is it a valid point of contention? No.

Most Millennials are products of the self-esteem movement, of limitless parental praise and schools whose goals were individual expression and personal happiness. Every morning, Mr. Rogers told them that they were special. All participants on athletic teams got medals. Everyone who did the work got As. Trying was as good as achieving.

Millennial workers are the result of this culture.

Gently disabuse them of the notion that they are the center of the universe, keeping in mind that even Aristotle got the planetary alignment wrong. If your patience is wearing thin, calculate the turnover cost per

Millennial employee, and then multiply it by those 8.6 jobs the average Millennial employee will have between the ages of 18 and 32.

Go one step farther. Turn the propensity for praise to your advantage. If they are motivated by praise, give it to them. Words are cheap.

Be aware of the flip side of praise: Criticism is not likely to be well taken. Or taken at all. It's that self-esteem thing again. One of the authors of this book, working as the assistant to the CEO of the biggest bank in the country, thought that instruction offered in conversational guise was optional, or at least open to discussion. Only after the CEO pointed out that the workplace was not a democracy did it sink in that ... the workplace is not a democracy.

When negative feedback is necessary, start with praise and give context for criticism. If the defensiveness card is played, don't trump it. It may take awhile to have objectively normal managerial conversations as many Millennials are not familiar with criticism.

Communicating with Millennials requires a new skill set. **They learn by always being connected, by multitasking, by sharing experiences using a wide range of communications technology and by co-creation.** In other words, Boomers learned the facts to pass the test. Millennials use experiential trial and error, constantly checking their network feedback, and create the learning experience.

Understanding this difference in learning styles will save jobs and organizational resources. Even better, be proactive: Have Boomers and Millennials coach each other, even if it's only a 90/10 or even an 80/20 overlap of understanding. They will leverage each other's strengths.

"Deloitte & Touche has implemented a training and career development and career management system that recognizes the primacy of learning as a core value of young workers. Managing the generational mix has resulted in hundreds of young workers staying at Deloitte with a declared savings of one hundred million dollars." [14]

The way that Millennials learn can directly benefit your organization in another way. Rapid change, relentless global competition and exploding complexity have turned even mundane decisions into problems of true uncertainty. *"A professional workforce used to 2-dimensional thinking now faces an n-dimensional world."* [15]

Millennials already live in complex imaginary dataspace, and are comfortable with handling a multitude of simultaneous data streams. Cutting edge analytic tools that explore real world "what if" scenarios – in finance, engineering, risk analysis, climate change - operate the same way that video games do. Using them is a purely digital, interactive experience. There is no bottom line, no final report. They create value by helping teams explore operational uncertainties.

They are the future in real time, delivered by the only generation that understands how to use them.

What Millennials don't understand is the workplace – its constructs, constraints and culture. All their lives they've had coaches for every physical skill, and mentors for every intellectual interest. In the workplace, they need guides to corporate culture, guides to bridge the generation gap, guides to interpret communication.

Boomers can step right into these starring roles.

How? It's useful to start by getting some solid information about the demographics of your organization. As in, **do a quick age profile** to make sure that you understand who's working for you. If you understand their various motivational profiles, you can implement ways to develop their skills, harness their energies, and promote mutual coaching. This will go a long way toward employee actualization, and avoid or minimize the substantial costs of conflicts and turnover, to say nothing of developing bench strength to cover Boomer retirements.

> *"Don't waste time wishing your Millennial employees were different. Don't spend your energy comparing today's youth to the desires and drive you had at age 18. These employees are not a reflection of you, nor are they an earlier version of you. That is okay. Your task is to take this new understanding and use it to reposition how you interact with, motivate, and reward your staff."* [16]

FUSIONS

- *Millennial attributes are neither right nor wrong, even when measured against Boomer expectations: They are just different.*
- *Understanding the difference in learning styles – Boomers learned the facts to pass the test, Millennials create their learning experiences – will reduce turnover and increase organizational resources.*
- *Do a quick age profile of your workforce to understand who's working for you and their various motivational profiles.*
- *Have Boomers and Millennials coach each other, even if it's only a 90/10 or even an 80/20 overlap of understanding. They will leverage each other's strengths.*

Chapter 2
Getting Them to Line Up At the Door
(Recruitment)

NASA Intern Hoping To Go On Space Walk Before He Leaves In June

⌘　⌘　⌘

"(Millennials) don't seek a job as much as they seek an opportunity. They have multiple expectations of an organization - it isn't just the job description but the workplace culture, the variety, fun, training, management style, and flexibility that drives them." [17]

How are you going to *get* these unparalleledly productive workers who will bring you 21st century innovation and profitability? By understanding, accepting and mirroring their key needs in your recruitment strategies so that they will swarm to your organization like bees to honey. And, of course, by looking for them where they're looking for you. *"If you are able to create an environment that embraces the strengths of Millennials, then you will become an employer of clear choice. You can't be chosen unless you're a choice."* [18]

How to Recruit Millennials

Understanding and being sensitive to their needs are the key factors in recruiting them. They are different from other workers. Accept that and move forward. If you want them to care about your organization, show them that you care about them.

Start with the first sentence of your job description. It has to hook Millennials, who won't read past it otherwise. It should explain why your organization is great and how it is making a difference in the community, the city, county, state, country, world or universe. The rest of the job description should detail how that job will position the Millennial for a successful career – not just with your organization.

> *"The old approach is to list all of the responsibilities someone will have when they work for you. But we Millennials aren't looking for a laundry list of things that you will tell us to do. We're looking for a reason to believe in your company. Give us one."* [19]

Respect them with a lean hiring process. There is no real need for multiple call backs and interviews other than disorganization. There is no need for a hiring decision to take months. Millennials don't wait for months.

Sell your people, not your company. Millennials are people-oriented. Introduce them to the cool people they'll be working with. Detail the stellar career paths of people who started with your organization and got into excellent graduate schools, or who got great jobs internally or elsewhere. The best people to connect with Millennials are other Millennials, who can let the newbie in on how the job really works.

> *"In looking for a job, then, my most important criterion has become the company culture. I want to know how employees interact, how comfortable it is to be in the same place every day, and how friendly the office environment is. Starting a new job is extremely intimidating. I want to work side by side with people who understand where I'm coming from. People I'll hang out with on evenings and weekends. To people my age, entering the workforce seems akin to landing on the beaches of Normandy, and as I venture into a new job I want to know that I'm there in the trenches with people I like and care about."* [20]

Keep their options open. Millennials want to take a job because they *want* to, not because they *have* to. They hate being trapped in boring jobs, or on a track they don't choose. Convince them that working for your organization is good for *anything* they want to do.

Make a Compelling Value Proposition. Offer money and benefits, plus a clear reason to join your organization, one that resonates with their priorities. [21]

Make them feel special. Millennials expect personalization, to minimize the robotic feeling of the recruitment process. Because they have grown up in a highly customized culture, where everything from iPod playlists to cancer treatments has been individualized, they expect recruitment to conform to their personal desires, as well. They may negotiate interview times. They expect courtesy notes thanking them for applying to your company. They expect you to know who they are, and what they have to offer.

Promise them intense, meaningful work. No organization can afford to waste resources on meaningless projects. Everyone has to contribute from the get go. Millennials love this. For them it's cool to contribute to the organization's goals immediately; otherwise they risk becoming a caricature from the movie "Office Space."

Highlight your technology. Millennials use technology for everything. Technology is a universal language, part Esperanto, part mathematical, part sign language. They learned it before they learned the sentence structure of their primary language. They learned how to sign on, toggle, navigate user interfaces and move up game levels before they could ride a tricycle. The authors' sons, now ages 25, 16 and 13, had email, PCs, video games, iPods and cell phones while they were in the single digits. They are each adept at all things technological, having learned how to think like designers and programmers by being constant users. They are now experience-based learners. They are digital natives, as described in Mark Prensky's groundbreaking work, *Digital Natives Digital Immigrants.* [22]

> *"During breakfast the other day, our six-year-old son, Lachlan, decided to make himself some toast. Grabbing a piece of bread, and on the point of placing it in the toaster, he said to his mother, 'Mum, how do I put the bread in – landscape or portrait?'"* [23]

Don't BS them. Millennials have excellent BS detectors. They'll know it if you shine them on. They'll leave you at the door.

Show EQ (emotional IQ). Coming from a child-centric culture, they have been asked how they <u>feel</u> about every aspect of their lives since being gently removed from their mothers' wombs by pre-scheduled caesarean section. They were not asked to suck it up when they lost, told that it's just life when things didn't always go their way, or sent to their rooms without dinner when they acted up. Instead, they were encouraged to express their feelings, and counseled by parents, teachers, coaches and therapists. Most of their interactions have been mediated: Try to find a Millennial who has settled an argument by a fistfight, or handled a disagreement with a teacher independently. Millennials want an emotional connection to their employer, their work and their colleagues. During the recruitment process, you can meet this expectation by establishing rapport and inquiring into their interests outside of the job. *"Stress the qualitative aspects of the company, its mission and any community work it does. Do some empathetic listening to your Millennial candidates, repeating their key points so that they know that you have heard them."* [24]

> *"Just as a business owner is concerned with the customer's emotional connection, he or she should also worry about the employee's emotional connection to the work experience."* [25]

Make a difference in the world. That's what these new workers are looking for, if not with your products or service, then in the community. Or ask them to help you go green. They'll love you for it – and get it done.

> As the authors of <u>Managing the Generation Mix</u> put it, Millennials demand *"the immediate gratification of making an immediate impact by doing meaningful work immediately."*
>
> - 67.4% of Generation Y believes that 1 or 2 interviews at the most are acceptable.
> - Only one in four Gen Y's would consider staying 5 years.
> - Employers should act quickly to stop candidates from taking another job. *"Their need to have things right away can cause them to accept another job just down the street after applying with you."* Do the interview on the spot, as soon as the application is filled out. Check the references right away, and be prepared to offer the job the next day. [26]

Where to Look for Millennials

Online Recruiting

No one is sadder than at least one of your authors that daily newspapers are on the top 10 list of disappearing daily pleasures, killed by plummeting advertising revenues. (The other thinks that it is high time for all media to go digital.) Advertisers of all kinds have fled to media that have larger key audiences. This is especially true of job recruiting, where huge Internet-based media such as Craigslist.com, Monster.com and careerbuilder.com rule. There are also specialty online recruitment sites for almost every industry, such as www.attorneyrecruitingspecialists.com for lawyers, as well as specialty sites focused on income, such as TheLadders.com, which advertises only jobs paying more than $100k/year.

Entire business models are built on the promise of online recruiting – at local, national and trade-related websites. At the macro level, Onrec.com, the North American Online Recruiting Magazine, has 4,593 recruitment sites in its complete database as of the summer of 2008. The Internet Recruiting Resource Center, recruitersnetwork. com/resources and business.com have hundreds of online resources free for employers, including quick tips, how-to articles, and videos. (You do know what resume spiders and robots are, don't you?) And of course there are literally thousands of blogs dealing with recruitment, such as 10 Must-Read Online-Recruiting Blogs. [27]

Social Networking Websites

The majority of Millennials apply for jobs online, which you might expect. You probably don't expect where. If you're using classified advertisements in newspapers or solely relying on online job boards, you're losing Millennial eyeballs. Since a majority of them link to each other through social networking sites, such as Facebook and MySpace, create an account on both and set up your own recruiting site on each. Assign a Millennial employee to update them often with what's hot in your organization, and what socially responsible issues you're involved with. Don't overlook LinkedIn, which describes itself as the world's largest professional networking site, with more than 24 million users representing 150 industries around the world. [28]

Corporate Electronic Job Boards

Most organizations know by now that they have to have an online presence (website), and that it has to have a career or job area geared for Millennials: cool, interactive and tech-oriented. You can amplify it with banners that showcase their interests, or place HR recruiting-specific banners in blogs that they frequent. McDonald's now has Internet-based job application kiosks in key locations, both because customers presumably will be familiar with the company's menus and mores, and also because of the convenience factor. The strategy is working: hiring at these locations is robust, and turnover has decreased 20%. [29]

Personal Networks

You are your own best recruiter. Use your own network of friends, neighbors, family, colleagues, vendors and acquaintances to find Millennial prospects, especially asking Millennials you already know if they have friends who fit your job requirements. Network their networks.

> *"Unique to this generation, the technological advances of their lifetimes have given them a jackpot of choices. The wealth of information available in milliseconds from the Internet, hundreds of television and radio stations to choose among and both suburban areas and cityscapes studded with megastores and malls have given (Millennials) the notion that if they do not get what they want from one source, they can immediately go to another. This means that they will question workplace policies and culture from dress codes to work schedules, and know that there are other options out there if they are not satisfied with the answers".*
>
> ⌘　⌘　⌘
>
> *"The war for talent is over and talent won."* [30]

FUSIONS

- Attract Millennials to your organization by under-standing, accepting and mirroring their key needs in your recruitment strategies ... and by looking for them where they're looking for you.
- Technology has given them a jackpot of choices: If they do not get what they want from one source, they can (and will) immediately go to another.
- Sell your people, not your company.
- Millennials want an emotional connection to their employer, their work and their colleagues.
- Since a majority of them link to each other through social networking sites, such as Facebook and MySpace, create an account on both and set up your own recruiting site on each.

Chapter 3
Speaking Their Language

> *"We really want to leverage and monetize our synergy with this new initiative, but there's a disconnect in terms of our reorg."*
>
> ⌘   ⌘   ⌘
>
> *"Blogs, Podcasts, Facebook applications, Mobile Apps, Google AdWords, Twitter, Desktop Widgets, FriendFeed, Orkut, RSS... . Everyone's talking about it – How to use new media technologies for a corporate or business use. Maybe it's to save money. Or make money. Whatever."* [31]

If you're a digital native, (definition = a person who has never lived in a world without computers, cell phones, iPods, etc.), the first sentence in the text box above will make you LOL (laugh out loud). Or gag. You will totally get the second one.

If you're a Boomer, the reverse will be true.

You are likely not using the same language.

Millennials have their own language, which is verbal, unstructured, abbreviated and tech-based. It is also global. They think mosaically.

What does that mean to you as an employer?

We are now employing the first post-literate generation. Or, as a recent *Atlantic* Magazine cover trumpeted, *"Is Google Making Us Stoopid?"* [32]

"Since Gutenberg's printing press, the spoken word was a more relaxed version of the structured written word - but the same basic rules of grammar applied. This has now changed. For the first time in the English language, we have a growing dichotomy between the written and spoken language. For Millennials, spoken terms are not intended to be written. And their written language has adapted to their technology via texting."

Communication for Millennials:

- All information is data: it has the same weight regardless of source (Wikipedia is more widely accessed than Encyclopedia Britannica)
- An electronic document is more current (and thus more accurate) than a printed page
- Speed is more important than accuracy
- DVDs are better than books
- A written word can be replaced by a PXT (picture text)
- A letter can be replaced by a text message complete with emoticons J and new forms of spelling 4u2c
- IM and email are more efficient than face-to-face meetings [33]

Millennials are far from illiterate (even though their grammar and spelling may leave you in doubt); indeed, they are the most educated generation in history. But for employers, the literate forms of communication alone won't connect today. It is a visual world. Millennials are a multi-modal generation, and you need to communicate in ways to engage multiple learning channels.

The more styles you use, the fewer Millennials you'll lose.

Learn their language – communicate in terms they understand. Communication begins with the graphics and snappy text you design to recruit them, extends through training materials which had better be animated and interactive, and works best through varied expression in presentations using flash rather than PowerPoint, blogs rather than white papers, video rather than text, and most definitely short rather than long. [34]

> *"Only 30% of Millennials are auditory. Today 70% are non-auditory learners, influenced by the visual nature of communication, and by kinesthetic, collaborative and interactive styles."* [35]

It should come as no surprise that lack of written communications skills is the #1 gripe of employers. You can demand that Millennials abide by the rules of grammar, spelling and scholarship that got you where you are. If you do, you will likely need to provide remedial language arts training, as many companies (and the US Army) have found out. Some organizations also require Millennials to give frequent verbal presentations to wean them from their dependence on electronic communication.

Talking the Talk

> "What's even more frustrating to some … managers is Millennials' total disinterest in 'sucking up' and tendency to bluntly tell the manger and other employees exactly what they think of a situation." [36]

As communicators, Millennials also tend to tell truth to power. In other words, they speak what's on their minds. And questions are their communications currency. Here's an excerpt from a recent interview with the Dean of the Haas Business School at the University of California, Berkeley:

Q: "(Candidates for admission call you to ask how to slant their applications). So obviously (Millennials) are not always thinking for themselves. As the gatekeeper for an MBA program, does that scare the daylights out of you?

A: Look, they're smart people. Whether I think it's good or bad really doesn't matter; it's clearly a generational issue and a market condition that I have to respond to. I like to think of it as an opportunity to help develop people who have a different style of communicating. Everyone who has contact with folks of this generation should view it as an *opportunity to help develop them into the kinds of leaders we want. The transparency that allows them to brazenly ask all of those questions is the kind of transparency they have about everything. In regard to government and corporate America, this generation's values are a very good trend. Hopefully it'll have an enormously positive impact."* [37]

If you want to learn more about how Millennials communicate (and think), access their media. Read *Wired* Magazine. Look at ypulse.com, MySpace and Facebook, secondlife.com, generationwhy.com, millennialsrising.com. Listen to top playlists on Apple's iTunes store. Or to blogtalkradio.com/Y-talk. Browse through YouTube.com.

> *"Y-Talk radio is dedicated to the latest, hottest news and interviews for Generation Y and those people who want to hire them, market to them, teach them and lead them. Each week, we feature some of the top Generation Y entrepreneurs, careerists, consultants and educators from around the world."* [38]

As for the new workplace language, there are many excellent and entertaining guides. McCrindle's "Word Up", Urbandictionary.com and Harry Newton's <u>Telecom Dictionary</u> are all great. One of our favorites is buzzwhack.com, for people who take pleasure in creating a new corporatespeak. Bookmark it. YWIA.

We loved these top 13 American buzzers [39] :

1. *Blamestorming: A group process where participants analyze a failed project and look for scapegoats other than themselves.*

2. *Death by Tweakage: When a product or project fails due to unnecessary tinkering or too many last-minute revisions.*

3. *BMWs: Bitchers, Moaners and Whiners.*

4. *Clockroaches: Employees who spend most of their day watching the clock - instead of doing their jobs.*

5. *Plutoed: To be unceremoniously dumped or relegated to a lower position without an adequate reason or explanation.*

6. *Prairie dogging: A modern office phenomenon. Occurs when workers simultaneously pop their heads up out of their cubicles to see what's going on.*

7. *Carbon-based error: Error caused by a human, not a computer (which we assume would be a silicon-based error).*

8. *Menoporsche: Male menopause. Symptoms include a sudden lack of energy, crankiness and the overpowering urge to buy a Porsche.*

9. *Adminisphere: The upper levels of management where big, impractical, and counterproductive decisions are made.*

10. *Deja poo: The feeling that you've stepped in this bull before.*

11. *Bobbleheading: The mass nod of agreement by participants in a meeting to comments made by the boss even though most have no idea what he/she just said.*

12. *Ringtone rage: The violent response by cube mates after hearing your annoying cell phone ringtone for the 15th time.*

13. *Muffin top: The unsightly roll of flesh that spills over the waist of a pair of too-tight pants.*

"Gradually, traditional communication methods are being ignored.... The shift is gradual because there is a new generation, Millennials are entering the workforce and they are wrecking havoc with traditional business communications." [40]

FUSIONS

- Millennials have their own language, which is verbal, unstructured, abbreviated, tech-based and global.
- They think mosaically.
- They are the first post-literate generation.
- Millennials are a multi-modal generation, and you need to communicate in ways to engage multiple learning channels. The more communications styles you use, the fewer Millennials you'll lose.
- If you want to learn more about how Millennials communicate (and think), access their media.

Chapter 4
Motivating and Keeping Millennials

"This (Millennial) generation is going to come to work with higher expectations than any other. They will be quickly disappointed if it's not as good as they had hoped. With one click of a mouse, they can tell thousands of other people, 'Don't come to work for XYZ company'."

⌘　⌘　⌘

"If we don't like a job, we quit." [41]

Now that your recruiting efforts have been successful, and you have a full complement of Millennials, the questions are how to keep them engaged, how to leverage their unique talents to the benefit of your organization, and how to keep them at all. Statistics show that the average Millennial works just 6 hours per day, has a job satisfaction rate of 20%, and has an average job tenure of 2 years. [42]

You can do better.

The key to motivating and retaining Millennials is to understand how they view the world and their role in your organization. If you've made the right moves recruiting them, you're well on your way to understanding what they want from you as an employer. **Millennials leave jobs not because there is a compelling reason to leave but because there is no compelling reason to stay.** They leave jobs because the work is not challenging and/or rewarding. They stay with organizations that promote their professional growth and provide personal satisfaction through respect, recognition and reward.

There are at least a dozen ways to motivate and retain Millennials:

1. Money
2. Mentors
3. Interesting work
4. Technology
5. Continual learning
6. Continual performance reviews
7. Connection
8. Flexible scheduling
9. Emotional intelligence
10. Social cause
11. Respect
12. Little things

Money Matters

As we detail in chapter 5, everyone works for money, no matter how idealistic they are, and this includes Millennials. Because they're young and inexperienced, the temptation is to pay them as little as possible. That is an excellent strategy if you enjoy high turnover. Millennials know how to get data, most especially salary ranges for comparable jobs. 2–3% annual raises will neither motivate nor keep them. In addition, theirs is not a long-term view: They may well require a higher starting salary knowing that promises of raises and promotions may never materialize, or that they may not be around to collect.

For optimal motivation, a smorgasbord of benefits should complement salary. Millennials value both traditional and customized non-traditional benefits: tuition and health club reimbursement; gift certificates to hip eateries; peer-nominated awards; time off for good behavior; music, movie and sports tickets; paid time off for community service. Consider awarding quarterly bonuses instead of, or in addition to, annual bonuses. Change long-term compensation incentive plans so that pay-offs take effect after shorter time periods. Provide longer vacations after shorter lengths of service. Above all, ask them what benefits and policies they would value. **You need to float their boat regularly: pennies raining down on their desk, or more frequent time off. They get bored with routine easily and need to decompress.**

Mentors and Managers

"We understand the importance of great mentors. We will teach our older co-workers about new technologies and the power of online communities, and they will respond kindly by guiding us through the insane office politics that exist everywhere." [43]

Mentors are crucial to Millennials. They have been coached their entire lives, from preschool through college. And, since by definition all Millennials are new to the professional workplace, they need mentoring, no matter how smart and confident they seem. **Mentors should introduce themselves <u>before</u> the new millennial employee begins work, and stick at least through the crucial first 100 days.** Millennials need to be engaged in what the business is all about immediately, from the moment the offer is given. If they were a college athlete, they certainly experienced fast onboarding in the college recruiting process.

Scheduled mentor meetings with affirmative information and suggestions work best. Instead of broad questions such as "How's it going?" let them know that what they do is important. Discuss specific goals in terms of concrete action steps, and offer resources and information. Share your own stories. Resist the temptation to parent. Because they work so well in team situations, consider mentoring Millennials in groups, so they can act as each other's resources or peer mentors. Talk to them about the business and how it makes money. Talk to them about the business and how it does good.

The goal of mentoring is to create future leaders who don't make the same mistakes you did.

> *"Before he left GE, Jack Welch had his top 1,000 managers be mentored by young GE employees, 'many of whom had just joined the firm, but who nevertheless understood the new technologies better than GE's finest.' Microsoft now sees the role of its managers as 'clearing obstacles from the paths' chosen by its programmers, often its youngest employees, who carry the firm's future products in their heads."* [44]

As for managing Millennials, one of our favorite maxims is, *"If you're leading, and no one's following, then you're just out for a walk."* (John Maxwell, leadership expert) Their ideal manager values communication and creates an environment of transparency and respect, is more consensus than command, more participative than hierarchical, more inclusive and participative, with demonstrated people skills as opposed to just job competence. [45] As gamers, they need explicit instructions, continuous assessments, and constant feedback. They thrive on instant gratification and frequent rewards. Communicate clear goals and expectations, then back off. Let them do projects their way so long as results are delivered your way.

Interesting and Meaningful Work

Millennials are a DIY (do it yourself) generation. Schooled by gamer technology, they operate at twitch speed, and learn by doing – often trial and error. Change is like the air they breathe. So work that involves variety, challenge, flexibility, and opportunity for advancement is critical. They want to learn, and like to participate in projects that give hands-on experience. Interest lies in making significant contributions to their organizations as they learn, and not waiting for someone to decide it's time for them to be seen and heard.

To really prime motivation, involve Millennials in direct contact with internal and external customers, so they better understand *why* their jobs are important and what's in it for *them*. For extra points you can emulate Google, embracing creativity and innovation by allowing employees one day a week just to invent new product ideas ☺.

As for meaning, we all need meaningful work. Through thousands of one-on-one interactions, researchers at the Institute for Labor and Mental Health found that socially meaningless work is a major cause of stress, and that *"most people have a real need for meaning and purpose in their lives... that transcends the competitive marketplace...."* [46]

For Millennials, that need is acute. Connecting work to meaning through discussion, example, and pay-it-forward-thinking is an emotional connection with your organization that benefits both parties.

Technology

Almost every business decision for almost every one of your constituencies is impacted by the rapid changes in technology today. This is where Millennials need the latest, and will make their greatest, contribution. Marc Prensky covers this point best: *"Digital Natives are used to receiving information really fast. They like to parallel process and multi-task. They prefer their graphics before their text rather than the opposite. They prefer random access (like hypertext). They function best when networked.... Their online life has become an entire strategy for how to live, survive and thrive in the 21st century, where cyberspace is a part of everyday life."* [47]

To keep Millennials engaged, give them tech tools to do their jobs. Use every imaginable technology – podcasts, vlogs and blogs, online brainstorming sessions, gamer software. Keep them focused on speed, customization and interactivity. They can't see the future, but they know where it is, and how to get there through technology.

"They communicate, share, buy, sell, exchange, create, meet, collect, coordinate, play games, learn, evolve, search, analyze, report, program, socialize, explore, and even transgress using new digital methods and a new vocabulary most older managers don't even understand. Blog? Wiki? RTS? Spawn? POS? Astroturf? How do these sound when juxtaposed with cross-functional cooperation, team-based management, and 360 feedback?" [48]

Continual Learning

The mantra of lifelong education combined with the cultural experience of constant change has led Millennials to require continual training in whatever job they hold. Their key to remaining relevant in changing times is on-going training, which will make them effective in their current job, and employable in future jobs which may be just a few years away. In a recent survey, 80% of Millennials polled stated that career development through additional training was very important to them. 90% agreed that regular training from their employer would motivate them to stay with an organization longer. Overall, they preferred "soft skills" (presentation, management and communication skills) as opposed to "hard skills" (technical training) which was seen as relevant only for a current job. [49]

> "They are focused on their own personal development. They want an accelerated path to success, often exaggerate the impact of their own contributions, are not willing "to pay the price," and have little fear of authority. As a result, they are often not a good bet for long-term employment, because they are quite willing to seek other employment (or no employment) rather than remain in a job in which they are not growing. They want their managers to understand their needs and lay out career options. In short, they are high maintenance, high risk, and often high output employees." [50]

Millennials will not read traditional written, static information for skill training or career development. Some organizations, especially high-tech companies such as Sun and Google, have recognized this, and have developed interactive electronic instruction. Companies with large numbers of blue collar Millennials have successfully combined hands-on with electronic instruction. UPS and the US Army are leaders in this area.

However you provide training, give opportunities to learn in a variety of media –on-line, via podcasts/ thumb-drives, over lunch-and-learns, from webinars, in classes, and from varied work experiences. Individual customization is key, as it is in coaching, mentoring and job rotations. Some organizations offer strength and personality assessment tools to increase self-awareness. [51]

We are often asked why organizations should spend the money on training if Millennials are just going to leave anyway. The answer is that **if you provide accessible training, Millennials will appreciate your organization, and have a higher probability of becoming intrapreneurs, who will run your business 10-20 years down the road.**

Continual Performance Reviews

Millennials want constant feedback. As one put it, *"If we're only at a company for two years, we cannot wait for our one year review to find out how we're doing. (We) will invent the on-the-spot performance review. Spot reviews lead to consistent improvement, and consistent improvement is what truly matters to (us)."* [52]

Whether or not you can stomach giving constant feedback, allow Millennials to request a performance review at any time during their first 90 days on the job. Whether for a long or a short term tenure, establishing a clear career track supported by a performance review process helps employees understand how they're doing and encourages them to keep improving and moving forward in your organization.

Work/life Balance

This is a faultline for Millennials, who like to work hard, but require a life of their own. Employment is a major part of their week, but it is not their life; it provides the funds to fuel their life. A career that allows them the opportunity to continue the other aspects of their existence – educational, social, spiritual, or entrepreneurial – is highly attractive. Employers who offer work schedule flexibility such as summer hours, flex-time or work-at-home programs will top the motivational top 10 list.

This is also a good place to note that Millennials are productivity machines. They will figure out how to get as much done in six to seven hours as the average boomer does in eight to ten. We suggest that you let them.

> *"When I signed on here, I never figured you were going to make me work the whole time."* [53]

Emotional Intelligence

Millennials are more psychological than other generations. As McCrindle researchers put it, *"For the 21st century generations, the educational and technological developments have had psychological impacts. When comparing (them) with previous generations... how decisions are made and how (they) are engaged have ... changed.... (Millennials) need to be engaged more on the emotive scale than the cognitive scale. They have been influenced not just by the scientific method but also by virtual reality. For them it is a world of experience – not just evidence. (In business, this is evidenced in) the shift in focus from IQ (intellectual intelligence) to EQ (emotional intelligence)."* [54]

What this means to their employers is that Millennials demand emotional validation in the workplace. Heart stuff, not head stuff. Managers need to connect on a non-intellectual plane, inquiring about Millennials' well-being and how they feel about their work. They have to manage people, not jobs.

Sociable Culture

High parental divorce rates combined with two working parents may have led Millennials to be more peer-oriented and more inclined to place a premium on workplace culture. [55] They want an environment where they can interact socially and work collaboratively, and enjoy being friends with co-workers. Creating office space that encourages co-workers to share ideas and interact with each other can promote this sociability and teamwork. This generation wants to look forward to going to work every day and wants to enjoy a fun, friendly and creative environment in which to work and grow as individuals.

Social Cause

Research suggests that Millennials want to work for organizations that are civic-minded and socially responsible. This means that the organization makes good products or services, gives back to the community, and is a good steward of the environment. Establishing a community service program that fits within your culture and making sure to communicate it to employees on the company's website, in job ads, interviews and company collateral heightens your profile and your worth as an employer. [56]

Respect and Appreciation

Those who study Millennials in the workplace seem to agree that respect and appreciation of Millennial ideas and work is a key motivator and retention factor. The more their work can be shown to be key to the resolution of a problem, retention of key customers, development of a new product line or the overall success of your organization, the more likely the work will motivate them and cause them to stay the course.

Look for rewarding opportunities. There cannot be too much public praise, or too many thank you notes, personal thanks, and small rewards from managers, especially if they recognize accomplishments as they are made. The world for Millennials has become incentivized. Customer loyalty is bought with frequent buyer programs, points, or discounts. So is employee loyalty.

Little Things

Beyond the top 11, it's the small things that can convince Millennials to play and to stay:

- Make their first day unforgettable
- Celebrate birthdays
- Give them business cards immediately
- Let them attend management meetings
- Create mentoring and social activities
- Create virtual network of peers, mentors, senior staff from the moment they darken the door
- Set up office spaces to encourage social interaction and exchange of ideas
- Assign work stations closer to more senior employees
- Hold only productive meetings

"Efficiency is the name of the game with Gen Y. We know that a drawn out meeting really means, "We have no idea what we're doing," and these time suckers actually halt productivity and stifle creativity, the qualities that they were supposed to encourage." [57]

> *"The future has arrived; it's just not evenly distributed."* [58]

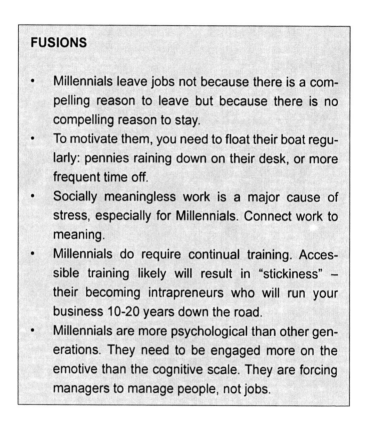

FUSIONS

- Millennials leave jobs not because there is a compelling reason to leave but because there is no compelling reason to stay.
- To motivate them, you need to float their boat regularly: pennies raining down on their desk, or more frequent time off.
- Socially meaningless work is a major cause of stress, especially for Millennials. Connect work to meaning.
- Millennials do require continual training. Accessible training likely will result in "stickiness" – their becoming intrapreneurs who will run your business 10-20 years down the road.
- Millennials are more psychological than other generations. They need to be engaged more on the emotive than the cognitive scale. They are forcing managers to manage people, not jobs.

Chapter 5
Rewarding Them

> "At first, the (Millennials) were the Children of the Rising Dow. They grew up during the greatest period of wealth creation in modern history, but watched their elders consume resources and run up deficits as if the party would never end. Then came the dot-com crash, terrorism, war, climate change. Epic uncertainty informs their worldview." [59]

For Boomers, salary and benefits have been the Holy Grail at the end of the road to retirement salvation. Every salary increase, no matter how modest, was something to celebrate. Each extra dollar funded current expenses, and compounded over time and accrued to our all-important retirement account. Increasing salary and incentive pay was the game to be played – in fact it was the only game around.

For Millennials, salary and benefits are not as important, or better put, they are not important in the same way. Millennial economic realities are different, as are their perspectives and lifestyles. There is a veritable smorgasbord of incentives and rewards on offer now in most companies, and the philosophy of pay – which had always keyed off of incremental increases – has changed radically to include not just pay for performance, but pay for potential.

Even though pay may not be a deal-breaker for them initially, earning potential still plays a role in whether to stay or switch employers. Getting into the minds of Millennials to come up with incentives that truly motivate, reward and keep them from job hopping is keeping many thousands of HR and comp specialists employed.

> For every 10 articles you read on Millennial compensation, 5 will say salary is key and 5 will say lifestyle and workplace accommodations are key. There is very good research to support both statements. Here's the scoop: **Millennials expect both.** They expect hard dollars and soft ego, lifestyle and workplace boosters.

The 411 on Millennial Financials

We are great believers in developing **unique motivational profiles** for each employee. This is in effect creating a flexible compensation program that recognizes the specific attributes, over time, of each employee. It is the creation of possibilities. This is especially important to do for Millennials who, as we have explained, have had totally customized interactions in every aspect of their lives. And yes, we know that it can be a nightmare in big organizations whose HR bureaucracies have outgrown their original purpose of employee service. We go into these companies all the time and help streamline and innovate compensation and benefits processes. So be of stout heart: It can be done. A key is to have employees manage their salary and benefits package components online, themselves – they are responsible for meeting enrollment period requirements, change forms, reading quarterly reports, etc. Millennials are especially good at this.

Here is some context on Millennial finances:

⌘ Many Millennials are operating under crushing debt loads from their educations: Most college students graduate with close to $20,000 in student loan debt. Graduate and professional students easily can incur $100,000 in loans that have to be repaid as of day one on the job. Knowledge economy workers, they have made great investment in higher education, whose costs have risen by 63% at public and 47% at private colleges in the last decade-and-a-half. [60]

⌘ Millennials now entering the workplace earn less than their counterparts did in previous generations. Most workers' real wages have been stagnant in the 2000's, especially since 2003, and the gap between productivity growth and workers' wages is at a historically high level. The inflation-adjusted earnings of new college grads have fallen 8.5 percent since 2000. [61]

⌘ Millennials' entry into the workforce has coincided with rapid increases in key living costs. Education, housing and health care costs have increased rapidly over the last decade. Rents have gone up 50% in major metro areas in the last 10 years. Even with home prices falling in many areas as a result of the mortgage crisis as this book goes to press, median home prices have skyrocketed in geographically appealing areas across the country, severely limiting affordability for first-time buyers. [62]

⌘ Millennials are paying more into Social Security than they pay in income taxes, even though most expect Social Security to be dead and buried long before they are – and long before they reach retirement age. [63]

"Overall, this year's batch of Undergrad participants expects to make $44,671 upon graduation and $74,752 after five years, and they expect a signing bonus of $6,308."

⌘　⌘　⌘

"There are many reasons for high turnover, but the most fundamental one is that baby Boomers have set up a workplace that uses financial bribes to get people to give up their time: Work sixty hours a week and we'll pay you six figures. (Millennials) will not have this. To hold out money as a carrot is insulting to a generation raised to think personal development is the holy grail of time spent well.... Our dream is about time, not money." [64]

It would be a mistake to think that Millennials do not care about salary. They do. In fact, where Boomers are more likely to want to be paid through a combination of salary and long-term savings and retirement options, as a whole, Millennials tend to prefer to receive immediate compensation for their contributions. Because of the drastic economic reversals they've seen in the business world, Millennials are cautious that neither they nor their organizations will be around long enough to reap the rewards of a pension plan or long-term savings options. They want a check and portable 401(k) match to make their own retirement-investment decisions.

Generational Differences

Popular thinking holds that:

- Millennials want fair pay, training opportunities that allow them to grow their careers and a flexible work schedule.
- Gen Xers desire work-life balance, immediate money (salary, 401(k) match) and plenty of vacation time.
- And Baby Boomers need benefit options for long-term care and want an admirable job title and responsibilities.

The crack in this perceptual framework is that it doesn't view the people in these groups as individuals. **In reality, you'll have to individually customize compensation plans to attract and create stickiness for young employees.** This isn't overly tough to do in concept, because it starts out with intuition: You can look at the workforce as a whole and see that older workers want respect and recognition in the form of titles and pay raises. Given where most of them are in their careers, that's not too surprising. Looking at younger workers' lives, you can see that they want to have more time away from the office, which isn't hard to understand. They're young, and they want to be out enjoying this time of their lives and doing things that are meaningful to them.

But intuition is not nearly enough. You have to do the research. We suggest that you simply **ASK your employees what they want**, and then provide it – within reason. This is not a revolutionary idea, although it seems to be a revolutionary practice. And it is difficult to execute, especially with a view to fairness across your employee base.

Consider the benefit of paid time off. Most employee surveys show that Boomers rank paid time off far lower than Millennials or Xers do. Of course they do. Most companies start employees – Millennials – with one week of vacation in the first year, and small increases as the years go on. Boomers, who've worked for decades, get 4-6 weeks of vacation. So Boomers neither need nor desire more paid time off.

So what happens if you decide to give Millennials – or any employee – the choice of additional time off? There are many ways to do this. The most obvious one is to trade salary increases for time off. Or flex time for increased responsibility. The bottom line is that soft incentives can be as valuable as hard cash. And, even if you're accommodating members of a particular cohort, make the accommodation available to everyone, and communicate it effectively.

This is a good place to put in a plug for **online HR materials**, especially salary and benefits information. Using online technology that can communicate the complete cost of employee compensation is a great educational tool that will actually be used. The cost to maintain an employee, including an itemization of salary and all benefits offered, can be automatically presented when employees log in to their employee accounts. This can be an eye-opener for all generations, but especially for those who are younger and may be less familiar with the cost of benefits plans. Online information helps you sell your organization's offerings. As important, you can solicit feedback on benefit plan offerings through online portals or surveys to determine if they are meeting employee needs – again, engaging employees by asking what they want. [65]

Companies that use compensation strategies most effectively seem to have two things in common: a willingness to be flexible with all levers of HR practices — including pay, benefits, and other perks — and the ability to make conscious attempts to understand, rather than assume, what drives desired employee engagement. [66]

Especially for Millennials, it's important to tie performance to compensation, shaped by individual employees' priorities. Millennials are merit-driven, and expect to be rewarded for their individual and team efforts. Again, you should consider all alternatives to compensating workers for a job well-done — not just increasing pay – particularly when another method might be just as effective or even better. Some companies do payroll every week instead of every two weeks, to help with cash flow for a generation that likes everything right away. This can also help reduce shrinkage, since an employee who runs out of cash is more likely to skim the register.

Non-Money Compensation and Incentives

> *"(Millennials) like money, are used to it, but they place a premium on their psychic income. They will be more attracted to employers that provide that psychic income. (Millennials) will choose workplaces and employers that provide an environment where they feel valued, have freedom to work on projects that are important to them, are recognized as individuals, and have opportunities to be mentored and to mentor others."* [67]

It seems true from the literature and anecdotal evidence that Millennials are most interested in advancing their skill sets. They want to be able to do it all and are willing to take an active role to develop and refine their skills. According to a recent SHRM Generational Difference survey, offering a range of benefits and training appeals most to them. They also value an organization that puts them on a clearly defined career path. So in designing your compensation packages, make sure to offer career development and training. [68]

Other benefits are less clear on the motivational front. Here is one survey ranking from HotJobs that shows a spectrum of benefits and how over 1,000 Millennial employees across the country ranked them on a scale of 1 to 10 in relation to their overall job satisfaction: [69]

Healthcare coverage	9.02
Vacation (paid time off)	8.82
Dental care coverage	8.80
401 (k)	8.58
Bonuses	8.25
Flexible working hours	8.06
Profit-sharing plans	7.52
Subsidized training/ed	7.51
Mentoring programs	6.41
Housing or relocation assistance	6.38
Free/subsidized snacks or	6.02
Subsidized transportation	5.73
On-site perks (such as dry cleaning)	5.59
Subsidized gym membership	5.59
Matching-gifts	5.33
Sabbaticals	5.26
On-site childcare	4.92
Adoption Assistance	4.05

Be aware that there's a danger in forming compensation strategies around generational categories because individual priorities will change over time, and there will always be exceptions. Nonetheless, we suggest that you offer a wide range of benefits covering all the option categories: concierge lifestyle, family friendly, flexible work schedules, work/life balance, discounts and cost savings, self-development, support, and profit sharing. [70] See what is used. Accommodate individual desires. It's worth the cost.

FUSIONS

- Millennials expect both hard dollars and soft ego, lifestyle and workplace boosters.
- For Millennials, salary and benefits are not as important as they have been to Boomers or, they are not important in the same way. Millennial economic realities are different, as are their perspectives and lifestyles.
- Develop a unique motivational profile for each employee, creating a flexible compensation program that recognizes the specific attributes, over time, of each. It is the creation of possibilities.
- <u>Ask</u> employees what they want.

The Bridge

> "Don't trust anyone over 30."
> 1964, Jack Weinberg, student at UC Berkeley
> (born 1940)
>
> ⌘ ⌘ ⌘
>
> "Don't trust anyone over 20."
> 2008, Stephen Hannan, student at Saint Mark's
> School (born 1995)

What we think Boomers need to know about Millennials in the workforce has covered five areas: definition, recruitment, communication, motivation and reward. Weaving these chapters together are the unique mindset and attributes of Millennials, which differ not just from those of Boomers, but from seniors, Xers, and everyone else occupying space in the workplace. Millennials are demonstrably different from other generations in their thinking, expectations, resourcefulness and results. They are paradoxically more psychological and less pragmatic than other generations at work. They do not perceive boundaries of time, space, age, gender, race, ownership or country of origin. They create their own learning experiences by being an integral part of the content. They favor random access over hierarchy or linearity. And they use technology the way the rest of us use breathing: to bring bodies of knowledge, modes of thought and ideas of abstraction to life.

We believe that these are the conditions necessary for true innovation.

The next five chapters tell Millennials about Boomers' workplace mindset, from the informed perspective that Boomers created the workplace as it exists. These chapters cover employer expectations, decoding the workplace and culture, compensation, workplace rules and regulations, and jobs in all their dysfunction. There is a huge amount of practical information in these chapters, often coated with humor, satire and perhaps a bit of parody. We hope that it is clear that Boomers bring enormous strength to the equation of 20th century workplace + 21st century workforce = creative economy. They provide knowledge, resources, stability and implementation skills. They model behaviors for Millennials from customer service to corporate responsibility. They are passionate about the social causes they embrace, as well as their generation's conviction that each person can make a difference. And they have proved that they can change the world, albeit pre-media 2.0: American Boomers ended the Vietnam war, pioneered racial parity, swept women into universities and workplaces, and explored outer space.

These generations must first understand themselves, and then understand each other. Mutual understanding between them is crucial because the relationship between them is the fuse that will ignite the full power of the creative economy.

"Unless you are a professional athlete or working on Wall Street, an entry-level salary is not very exciting.... I am not foolish enough to believe a paycheck will ever make me rich. The only reason I get excited about a 3% raise is because of what it represents: my hard work." [71]

Talking to Millennials

"Today we have a situation similar to ancient times when only a few people (known as scribes) could read and write. If you needed to send a letter, you went to a scribe, who created it for you. Today, if you need a software program to do something, such as collect political contributions online, you go to a Digital Native programmer, who can create whatever you need, from a website to a program, often in a matter of hours." [72]

⌘   ⌘   ⌘

"That's where Glassdoor.com comes in. It's US magazine for the company you are considering—a little gossipy, with first-hand information about companies from the people who suffer in them. Bonus: Glassdoor is a new company and there are not a lot of competing perspectives on the site yet. So if you drop a bomb about the place you work, it'll hit hard." [73]

⌘   ⌘   ⌘

"Damn! Mad props to her – mad props! I'm so proud of her!"

17-year-old classmate talking about 98-year-old Josephine Belasco, who was about to receive her diploma from Galileo High School, 80 years after dropping out. [74]

Chapter 6
Becoming the Perfect Plug 'n Play
(What Do Employers Want?!?)

> "The employer generally gets the employees he deserves." [75]

Google had 443,000 results for "perfect employee" when we began researching this chapter. That really narrowed down the 17,700,000 it had for "career advice". Other than finding your soul mate, what employers want seems to be the most thoroughly dissected subject in human history.

Fortunately, much of that wisdom can be neatly distilled and displayed. **For profit-making organizations, employers are looking for people who will help them make more money than they will cost.** This is true whether the organization is Boomer or Millennial oriented, whether the welcome sign is for creatives or accountants. For an organization to keep its doors open, it has to bring in enough money to pay the bills. [76] **For nonprofits, employers need externally-focused, future-oriented passion for the cause the nonprofit exists to serve.**

Skills Employers Want

So what does that mean to you as a prospective or current employee? Every job has specific requirements re: education and training, whether you're entry level or

C-level, IT or HR. You either have those requirements or you don't. Specific job requirements aside, there are broad ability skills that are crucial to your employment at every stage of your career.

Here are our **top 10 skills** most sought after by employers:

1. Messaging
(Communications – listening, verbal, written)
By far the #1 desired skill: communicating clearly and honestly with peers, managers and customers – to listen, write, and speak effectively.

2. Figuring it out
(Analytical/Research)
Accurately assessing situations, seeking other perspectives, gathering more information, identifying key issues.

3. Leveraging technology
(Computer/Technical Literacy)
True technological literacy means more than proficiency. The skill of putting numbers in a spreadsheet is manipulating data; the need is for data management. The skill of making memorable PowerPoints takes more than inputting words on slides; it begs for MP3 files, video, flash, hyperlinks, interactive graphics....

4. No boxes
(Flexibility/Adaptability/Managing Multiple Priorities)
Multitasking, setting priorities, adapting to chang-

ing conditions and work assignments, accepting new ideas.

5. Connecting
(Interpersonal Abilities)
Relating to colleagues up and down the chain of command, persuading others to participate, and mitigating conflict with co-workers.

6. Doing through others
(Leadership/Management Skills)
Taking charge and managing co-workers to meet goals.

7. Respect
(Multicultural experience/sensitivity/awareness
Multilingual ability)
Sensitivity and awareness of other people's differences and cultures; sharing your own differences and culture.

8. Time
(Planning/Organizing)
Planning, organizing, completing work and goals on time.

9. Solutions
(Problem-Solving/Reasoning/Creativity)
Solving problems using creativity, reasoning, experiences plus real-time resources.

10. Collaboration
(a/k/a Teamwork)
Working with others to achieve a common goal.

> *"Into being challenged? Into having fun? Want to change the world?*
> *If the answer is yes, then you've come to the right place…. As Google expands its development team, it continues to look for those who share an obsessive commitment to creating search perfection and having a great time doing it."* [77]

Values/Character Employers Want

Employers also want whole people. Equally important to hard and soft skills are the values, personality traits, and personal characteristics that consistently appear on 21st century employer must-have lists.

Here are the top 11 personal attributes wanted by employers, in order of completely arbitrary importance:

1. **Self-management**
2. **Personal accountability**
3. **Results orientation**

Self-management means that you know how to get things done … you don't just react to events, you plan for ways to make things happen ... you schedule your own time and your own energy ... you don't blame others ... you keep things from falling through the cracks ...you keep working until the job is done, without supervision... you know how to minimize interruptions and time wasters ... you make note of any promises you make and deadlines you agree to ... you do what you say you are going to do ... and you do it on time.

Personal accountability means owning up to your own actions. Even if the expectations aren't clear, you make decisions to the best of your knowledge, and take actions accordingly. You follow your conscience. If you make a mistake, you accept responsibility for it. You don't make excuses for bad decisions and you look hard for the root cause of flawed decisions so that you can learn from the experience.

Results orientation refers to the ability to meet schedules, deadlines, quotas, and performance goals. A person with a strong results orientation will favor tasks in which the outcome is achievable in a fairly short period of time. This is also known as keeping score. [78]

4. **Honesty/Integrity/Morality**. Employers probably respect personal integrity more than any other value, especially in light of the many recent corporate scandals.

5. **Dedication/Hard-Working/WorkEthic/Tenacity**. Employers seek job-seekers who love what they do and will keep at it until they solve the problem and get the job done.

6. **Dependability/Reliability/Responsibility.** There's no question that all employers desire employees who will arrive to work every day - on time - and ready to work, and who will take responsibility for their actions.

7. **Loyalty.** Employers want employees who will have a strong devotion to the company – even at times when the company is not necessarily loyal to its employees.

8. **PositiveAttitude/Motivation/Energy/Passion.** The job-seekers who get hired and the employees who get promoted are the ones with drive and passion – and who demonstrate this enthusiasm through their words and actions.

9. **Professionalism.** Deals with acting in a responsible and fair manner in all your personal and work activities, which is seen as a sign of maturity and self-confidence; avoid being petty.

10. **Self-Confidence.** Look at it this way: if you don't believe in yourself, in your unique mix of skills, education, and abilities, why should a prospective employer? Be confident in yourself and what you can offer employers.

11. **Willingness to Learn.** No matter what your age, no matter how much experience you have, you should always be willing to learn a new skill or technique.

Jobs are constantly changing and evolving, and you must show an openness to grow and learn with that change. [79]

Can you do the job?
Will you do the job?
Will you get along well with others?
Are you manageable?
Can the company afford you? [80]

And there are a few more values/character attributes that we have found useful in our careers, training and consulting work: [81]

Willingness to share information and ideas.

Ability to work under pressure.

Willingness to take calculated risks, without fear of consequences.

Understanding of business strategy and how you create shareholder value.

"Fact is, the work place to a great extent is where we live.... So good sense and good business and good engagement throughout the supply chain, from vendor's vendor to customer's customer, would benefit mightily—including on the P & L—if we insisted (!) on: Pleasant ... Caring ... Engaged." [82]

Privacy Is an Illusion

Employers Do Background Checks

Hiring is serious business. Each hire can, quite literally, be a million dollar decision if you look at average employee costs over an average career span. To hedge their bets and tilt the odds in favor of an excellent hiring decision, employers have a variety of selection tools at their disposal: starting with stated qualifications, such as GPA and technical proficiency; extending to interview questions designed to trap the unwary and throw them back into the unemployment pool; and culminating in a thorough look into your public records and recorded private life. Especially since 9/11, background checks themselves have become a billion dollar business.

So be aware that it is very likely that prospective employers will do a background check on you. Background reports can range from a verification of an applicant's Social Security number to a detailed account of the potential employee's history and acquaintances. Many employers are now searching MySpace and Facebook for the profiles of applicants. And note that almost as many **employers have searched such sites for information about current employees.** [83]

Here are some of the pieces of information that might be included in a background check. [84] Many are public records created by government agencies.

Driving records ... Vehicle registration ... Credit records ... Criminal records ... Social Security number ...

Education records ... Court records ... Workers' compensation ... Bankruptcy ... Character references ... Neighbor interviews ... Medical records ... Property ownership ... Military records ... State licensing records ... Drug test records ... Past employers ... Personal references ... Incarceration records ... Sex offender lists

Be acutely aware that in the age of media 2.0, **THERE IS NO PRIVACY**. Act and record accordingly. If you have subpar credit, have been convicted of a crime or have failed a drug test, be prepared to discuss the circumstances and lessons learned if the subject is brought up. Vet your profiles on social networking sites. If you have pictures or random thoughts or even links that would embarrass your mother, they can kill your chances with a prospective employer.

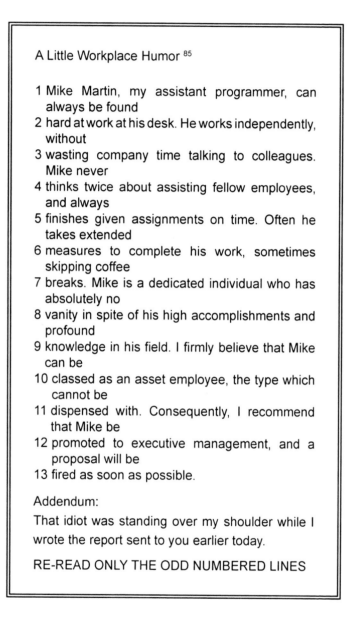

A Little Workplace Humor [85]

1 Mike Martin, my assistant programmer, can always be found

2 hard at work at his desk. He works independently, without

3 wasting company time talking to colleagues. Mike never

4 thinks twice about assisting fellow employees, and always

5 finishes given assignments on time. Often he takes extended

6 measures to complete his work, sometimes skipping coffee

7 breaks. Mike is a dedicated individual who has absolutely no

8 vanity in spite of his high accomplishments and profound

9 knowledge in his field. I firmly believe that Mike can be

10 classed as an asset employee, the type which cannot be

11 dispensed with. Consequently, I recommend that Mike be

12 promoted to executive management, and a proposal will be

13 fired as soon as possible.

Addendum:

That idiot was standing over my shoulder while I wrote the report sent to you earlier today.

RE-READ ONLY THE ODD NUMBERED LINES

FUSIONS

- For-profit organizations are looking for people who will help them make more money than they will cost.
- For nonprofits, employers need externally-focused, future-oriented passion for the cause the nonprofit exists to serve.
- Understand the business strategy and how you can help create value.
- There is no privacy. Many employers search MySpace and Facebook for the profiles of applicants – and current employees. Vet your profiles on social networking sites or secure access for friends only.

Chapter 7
80% of Success Is Showing Up and Other Career Myths Busted
(Decoding the Workplace and Its Culture)

Film maker Woody Allen is credited with saying that 80% of success is showing up. Steve Jobs said that it's better to be a pirate than to join the Navy. And business writer Hal Lancaster has suggested that getting fired is nature's way of telling you that you had the wrong job in the first place.

What do these sayings have in common (besides some humor)?

A grain of truth. And a lot of myth. This chapter takes a look at common workplace myths that can hamper Millennials' peace, productivity, promotion and prosperity.

> *"It's not who you are underneath but what you do that defines you."*
> Batman Begins, 2005

Top 12 Workplace Myths
As commonly misunderstood by Millennials

12 **You have to like your job to be happy.**

Likely yes. You spend 3/4 of your waking hours at work. So liking that time is pretty important. **But** the correlation between your happiness and your job can be overrated. The most important factors for happiness are strong personal relationships and meaningful life activities. If you have great friends and family, you can probably be happy even if you hate your job. (Imagine a portable toilet cleaner who's in love, or someone in a so-so job who spends free time volunteering at a community food bank.) But truly, if you hate your job, you should leave it.

---

*"Happiness, ventured William James, the noted 19th century philosopher/psychologist, is reflected in the ratio of one's accomplishments to one's aspirations. This suggests, of course, that when it comes to feeling happy in our lives, we can choose one of two paths: continually add to our list of accomplishments—**or lower our expectations**."*

⌘   ⌘   ⌘

"According to a study conducted by The Conference Board in 2005, Americans are increasingly unhappy with their jobs:
—Only 14% claim to be very satisfied.
—50% say they're dissatisfied.
—25% say they're just showing up for the paycheck." [86]

---

11 The glass ceiling doesn't exist.

YES it does. Our Millennial reviewers asked what the glass ceiling is. The answer is that it is a barrier to upward mobility formed by the prejudice of those in charge against those who are not like them. It is usually shorthand for male bosses keeping female workers in low-paying, nonexecutive jobs. NEWSFLASH: Women do not have the same opportunities for advancement as men. The Fortune 500 CEO list has two females. The Boards of Directors of the Ink 1000 include only a handful of females. Women still make only 77 cents to every male dollar. You do the math. While you're at it, try to find executives of major firms who are people of color, gay or lesbian, disabled, etc. They are rarer than hen's teeth. **Millennials can change this.**

10 The hardest workers get promoted.

Nope. The <u>most likable people get promoted</u>. Your mother was right: Good social skills are crucial to your career. Across the board, people would rather work with someone who is likeable and incompetent than with someone who is skilled and obnoxious. As Tiziana Casciaro of Harvard Business School says, *"How we value competence changes depending on whether we like someone or not."* Besides, people lacking social grace seem to lack other competencies, as well. Our advice is to read <u>Emotional Intelligence</u> by Daniel Goleman.[87] It will tell you everything you need to know.

9 Everyone has sex in the office.

Sorry, no. Everyone *thinks* about having sex in the office, but many people allow their forward brains to take precedence in the office setting. However, many, if not most of us can chalk up an office romance or two. And why not? The workplace offers opportunity (boys and girls together), motive (anti-boredom), and geographic convenience (employees will live within a reasonable distance of the office). And in fact, forty-one percent of employed Americans ages 25-40 have admitted to having engaged in an office romance, according to a joint survey sponsored by *Glamour* magazine and Lawyers.com. [88] Here's the kicker: Employers had the most problems with romance when a manager dated a reporting staff person. And the specter of sexual harassment is always present, especially once the affair is over. [89]

8 Office politics is about backstabbing.

NOT. Some long knives will be out wherever you go. But office politics is about helping people get what they want. Figuring out what they care about, and how to help them get it, obviates the need to strong-arm, disparage or manipulate co-workers. This does not mean that you can bare your soul to colleagues and expect your confidences to be kept, any more than you would expect that in a random group of acquaintances. Jealousy will still rear its ugly head. Use your judgment.

> *"Genius is one per cent inspiration, ninety-nine per cent perspiration."*
>
> ⌘   ⌘   ⌘
>
> *"It's not the hours you put in your work that counts, it's the work you put in the hours."* [90]

7 Do good work, and you'll do fine.

Nope. No one knows **what** you're doing in your cube if you're not telling them. Let people know what you're working on, and its success – especially your manager and manager's manager. No one else will do it for you. Recognize that self-promotion is an art form, and don't oversell.

6 A great resume will get you hired.

No. Only 10% of jobs come from sending unsolicited resumes. Most jobs come from people leveraging their networks. When you make a connection with a prospective employer, your resume will be glanced at to make sure there are no obvious problems (like not having the required skills). Expand your network instead of obsessing over which descriptive adjective best describes your PowerPoint skills. And NEVER lie or experiment with the truth on your resume. You will be found out and fired.

> "A former boss used to tell me that you should always hire A players because one B player brings everyone down – teams perform to their lowest performer. I think that's true. I also think that when an A sees a B on the team, the A doesn't want to come." [91]

5 It's better to emulate Donald Trump than to be yourself.

Nope. According to Guy Kawasaki, the magic formula to having a great career is to **be yourself** and to keep learning. Figure out how to do what you love, follow your heart's desire, and you'll be great at it. *"Those who stand out as leaders have a notable authenticity that enables them to make genuinely meaningful connections with a wide range of people."* [92]

---

3 Biggest Large Company Lies [93] :

- We have an entrepreneurial spirit here.
- People are our greatest resource.
- We say, let the marketplace decide.

3 Biggest Small Company Lies:

- We have an entrepreneurial spirit here.
- The boss is just one of the guys.
- Staying small is a conscious decision.

---

4 Millennials don't work for the money, but for the fulfillment.

Nonsense. Ask yourself this again: If you won the lottery tomorrow, would you go back to your day job the next day? Work is about money – see chapter 8. Money is about freedom to make life choices.

3 Email is always the most efficient communication method.

NO! Email has become so prevalent in the workplace that it's hard to remember a time without it. As its popularity has grown, so has overreliance and misuse. If you're explaining a complex procedure to a co-worker that requires multiple cycles of emails, you're losing time and straining patience. Calling or having facetime minimizes confusion and builds relationships. Without visual and aural cues, people often misinterpret emails' intent and message, even if you use those moronic emoticons (☺ – which is why they were invented). Face-to-face rules, voice is good, email is third choice. [94]

> *"There used to be website called Boomer Death Watch, that, as the name implies, kept track of deaths among prominent Baby Boomers such as the Chicago 8 and other Sixties notables. The animus — it's not only fair to call it that, it's the only thing you can call it — wasn't limited to counter-culture icons. As the site's motto went, 'Because one day they'll all be dead'."* [95]

2 There is a generation gap between Boomer bosses and Millennial workers that hampers productivity and the pursuit of workplace happiness.

Maybe yes, maybe no. We argue strongly that it's not a gap, it's a mashup. Clearly, people of different ages see the world in different ways, and bring different experience and skills to the proverbial table. Lassoing those skills to get that bronco moving forward with all of its energy intact is the goal. It's like any other relationship issue. If you ignore it, the relationship will fail. Some observers suggest that we need to look at power - who wields it and who wants it. *"The so-called generation gap is, in large part, the result of miscommunication and misunderstanding, fuelled by common insecurities and the desire for clout."* [96]

1 You can have it all. The biggest myth of all.

Absolutely not. Here's how it works: You can have the things you want most intermittently. That means that sometimes your job comes first. Sometimes your family. Sometimes you. They will never line up like bars on a slot machine. Chasing this dream will ruin you.

> *"Of course, it is very important to be sober when you take an exam. Many worthwhile careers in the street- cleansing, fruit-picking and subway-guitar-playing industries have been founded on a lack of understanding of this simple fact."* [97]

FUSIONS

- "It's not who you are underneath but what you do that defines you."
- The most likable people get promoted (not the hardest workers).
- Be yourself. Really.
- Without visual and aural cues, people often misinterpret emails' intent and message.
- You cannot have it all. You can have the things you want most, intermittently.

Chapter 8
Show Me the Money
(Compensation)

> "For Baby Boomers, the workplace competition was about money, and the material things that represent one's earnings…. But (Millennials) see the competition as about fulfillment, and they are determined to get it." [98]

We all work for money. No matter what else lures us into the workplace, no matter how our souls are salved by good deeds, our egos are massaged by visible praise, our need for companionship is met by fellow toilers, it is lucre that forces us away from World of Warcraft, YouTube, the Shopping Channel and filling our 160-gig iPods with more Metallica.

We'll make this point one more time: If you won the lottery tomorrow, would you go back to your day job? We always ask this question at some point in our presentations. Even the odd priest in the audience has looked thoughtful. The rest of us mere mortals say they'd quit in a New York minute if the financial necessity of working was eliminated. This holds true from geezers to Millennials.

But the importance of money is a matter of degree. To the Boomers, including the authors of this book, money paid our family expenses in single-earner families, it served as a marker to measure us against our peers, it paved the way in our lock-step promotions, and it was absolutely necessary to fund our retirement. There just wasn't much else in the limited range of compensation to be had. Millennials tend to think of pay as a naturally-occurring, direct result of appreciated individual work. It is an immediate causal after-effect of work in the moment. There is little expectation and little patience for long-term incremental rewards, but great expectation and great eagerness for rewards outside the monetary pay scale. And work/life balance is crucial.

How does this play out in today's workplace? Say you've got your Millennial dream job in sight. OK, you've got **a** job in sight. What's it worth to you? What's it worth to your potential employer?

The first thing to do is understand your organization's total compensation system or, failing access to it, a hypothetical compensation system. This will include everything from compensation philosophy through various kinds of pay and incentives and benefits to intrinsic rewards that make you feel good about what you do every day.

"*Gone are the days of working for a company for 30 to 40 years. In today's environment, nobody trusts the system to take care of them long term. From the collapse of Social Security to the fall of major companies during the dot-com era and, more recently, the Enron scandal,* **(Millennials) are acutely aware that nothing is a 'sure thing.'** *...(They) are, in a strange way, more in sync with the reality of today's economy than other generations because they've never known it any other way....If you don't trust the system to take care of you in the long run, you walk in the door looking to your immediate boss to take care of you in the short term."* [99]

Compensation Philosophy: Pay for Performance vs. Pay for Potential

You also need to know which compensation philosophy your organization uses: pay for performance or pay for potential.

Pay for performance is what the Boomers typically use to set and increase compensation. Everyone and every job is grouped together by function. The average salary increase is 3% annually. Seriously. Here is a graphic:

Why Pay for Performance Doesn't Work:
The Merit Increase Matrix Game [100]

	Rating	Position in Range by Quartiles – Minimum to Maximum			
		Min to 1st Q	1st Q to Mid	Mid to 3rd Q	3rd Q to Max
5	Wonderful	*Must walk on water and talk to higher powers.*			
4	Fantastic	*Too low to hire here **	6%	5%	*They never max out ***
3	Great		5%	4%	
2	Not so great	*Very few people rated here – hard to have the "tough conver-*			
1	Whoa!	*sations" with employees*			

Facts:

1. Average salary increase for the past 20 years = 4% +/- 2%

* No one hires at the minimum of the range; they hire around the 1st quartile

** Artificial promotions here to new job titles when people are too high in the range

*** The zone. 80% of all people are rated in these 4 cells; 1–2% differential between cells

2. Average worker makes $50,000

3. So 2% = $1,000; divide by 24 pay periods and calculate on an after tax basis....

4. Comes out to a 6-pack of beer

5. Pay for performance? Not!

Pay for potential is a compensation philosophy that tries to level the playing field based on what you bring to the job and how well you leverage those competencies. It's a new concept that gets rid of *"the more years you work the more money you should make"* mentality, and recognizes your talent and potential. While it is challenging for the Boomers to accept as a new way to think about compensation, it is far and away the best plan to connect and engage with Millennials.

Here's how it works. Say you've been writing computer programs since you were 12 and have a few video games that you've created as well. Why are you being paid less than a person who has 10 years fewer experience than you do? Because your talent and potential do not count in the 20th century workplace – until you demonstrate them through performance. And look how performance gets rewarded (see above Pay for Performance). If your organization has moved into the 21st century and believes in pay for potential – rewarding you for the skills and competencies that you bring in and how those unique assets get manifested in your work regardless of your age or years of workplace experience - then you may get your salary actually to reflect your true gifts.

Fundamentals of Making Money at Work
(a/k/a your Total Compensation Package)

The Corporate Buzz. Start by figuring out where your organization's head is at regarding how you get paid. Besides pay for performance vs. potential, do they want to motivate you to perform or just pay you for showing up? Or are they trying to get you to work your buns off for as cheap as they can – knowing that right before you leave, you'll sound off about pay and they can adjust your salary a little then? Know their M.O. - before and after you join them.

Paying the Bills. So what will they offer you for the basics – showing up, doing your job, producing some results? This is your **base salary.** They will spend a lot of time trying to figure out what you are worth in the marketplace, comparing your job to other jobs. The truth is, there is a lot of variability in the market depending on location, supply and demand and the skill set required. The more skills you have, the more you should get paid. Pay is an art form – not a science. Translation? You have plenty of room to negotiate – if you are good.

Understand that your initial base salary is what ALL future raises and salaries will key off of. Pay attention to this, as money earned is cumulative, as in lifetime earnings, social security payouts, benefits including retirement contributions. Throughout your working years, you've got to keep leveraging your salary, moving it up at every opportunity.

Pennies Raining Down on Your Desk. So when you do well, what happens? What are the motivational programs designed to recognize your accomplishments? Will pennies rain down on your desk? These are the **incentive** or **bonus programs.** Incentive derives from the

Latin "incendere" which means "to kindle or to incite". Organizations use many different types of programs – from annual incentives to holiday bonuses; from commissions (for sales people) to gainsharing (based on making money - profits or expense management). Whatever the program, do you know how much you'll get and for doing what? If not, ask!

A Piece of the Rock. The holy grail of making money has been **stock in the company**. If the company grows in value because of the work that you (and your friends) do, you should grow in value, too! This is a complicated area which has employed thousands of accountants, attorneys and consultants to design, communicate and, in short – figure out! So here is the Readers' Digest version of some stock programs:

- Stock Options – you get a price now to buy a piece of the rock later; you see how everything goes (does the stock go up or down?) and decide later whether you want to buy at that price.
- Restricted Stock – you get a piece of the rock now but what you can do with it is restricted for a period of time, usually based on your length of employment (service).
- Phantom Stock – you get something that looks, feels and acts like stock – but you can't vote it (like real owners). However, when the value of the real stock of the company goes up – phantom stock does, too!

Body, Mind and Spirit. For when you think you are burning out, or feel as if you are burned out, or you do burn out – the company has a program for you! Often referred to as **benefits,** these programs provide health insurance, vacation, and other paid time off – such as leave and holidays. Check these out – this will give you a pretty good indication as to an organization's culture and values.

Saving Money for Later. Do you think that retirement is so far away that you don't want to think about it now? So did the authors of this book. Unfortunately, time moves pretty quickly, so socking away money now for use later is a good idea. Your organization probably has something called a 401(k) plan or some other form of deferred compensation. In short, these programs allow you to put away money now for use later. Don't get hung up on all the tax consequences – the good news is if your organization sponsors a plan like this, it usually does so by matching your contributions up to a certain dollar amount. This is free money. Take it. Even if your employer doesn't offer a retirement plan, the government does, kind of, so sock some of your earnings away with an IRA, which can give you a tax deduction and tax-free earnings. You'll be glad you did well before you're a Boomer!

Melting Your Butter. In addition to everything mentioned above, what does your organization do to tell you how wonderful you are and to recognize what you have done for them? Do they:

- Provide additional time-off?
- Recognize you publicly?
- Give you constructive feedback on a regular basis?
- Give you the best post-graduate education (and development opportunities) you could possibly get?

The second thing to do is to understand that all components of pay are negotiable.

And that you are the chief negotiator. Think of it as free agency. How did A-Rod get that record-breaking salary?

You need to do some market research. These sites will give you an idea of what a person in your region, with your job, and with your job title might make:

- Salary.com – Great site: pay scales tend to be high
- Payscale.com
- Monster.com
- Are You Being Paid Enough? Take the Tickle. com Quiz

If you're looking for a job, armed with salary range knowledge, you go into your job interview. You're asked what salary range you have in mind. **Do not answer.** Ask nicely to defer the answer until you've discussed the job a bit more. Let the interviewer suggest a figure. Nod wisely. Do not snap at that lure like a hungry bass. Tell the interviewer that your research has shown the range for the job to be whatever it is, and that you believe your experience qualifies you to come in at the top of the range. You won't get it, but you'll probably get a counter offer somewhere in between.

Or maybe you're already parked in a cubie, wondering if you can sleep there if your paycheck doesn't cover the rent. Do you believe your work is worth more money than you're making? If so, you've got company. According to the most recent Salary.com survey [101] of 13,500 random site visitors, 65 percent of respondents said they're looking for a new job within the next three months. Fifty-seven percent of those say they're looking because they believe they are underpaid.

Again, do the market research on comparable jobs in your region.

Additionally, the HR department may have a regional salary range book. Ask if you can see this – it will be more accurate on what employees in your region make than the big national website employer surveys. Bigger organizations, as well as public entities, publish their pay ranges for all jobs. Ask! [102]

> "*Employers known for generous employee benefits may find (Millennial) workers indifferent to their offerings. Benefits are just a list of features; like what you would see on a car. No single element is going to stick out enough unless the benefit is profoundly different from anything else in the marketplace.*" [103]

Pay Raises

Compensation experts will tell you that pay raises depend on:

- Your industry,
- the market and market pay for your job in your region,
- the pay practices of your organization, and
- your performance on your job

All of that is true. What is also true is there are some **cheats** – just as in any game. Here are some:

- Know how your organization makes money. Whatever else you do, align your work with some part of that process.
- Document your contributions to the goals of your organization.

- Be aware of company policy regarding compensation. Some are limited by budget constraints, or can only give raises at certain times of the year.
- Have a clear idea of what you want. Determine the salary range you're looking for and justification for the increase and have both ready to roll.
- Be flexible. How about an extra week of vacation instead of a raise? Or a leave of absence to work for a cause that means a lot to you? Or to start a new project you've devised in your own organization?

Related Subjects

Job-hopping: Pros & Cons

Should you stay and suffer or bail when you're feeling pinched?

Pro: Pay increases. The best way to make a large jump in pay is to jump from one organization to another.

Pro: Networking. New jobs expose you to new networks of people, which can be useful and fun.

Pro: New skills. OTJ (on the job) training can teach new skills quickly.

Con: Going down. Your new job might be worse than your old job.

Con: Moving too soon. If you leave too quickly, you may not be getting everything your current workplace has to offer in terms of job skills, pay, networking, education, etc. Sometimes you have to put in time to get the benefits.

According to the US Labor Department, most people will have eight jobs between the time they are eighteen and thirty. This means that most Millennials are job hopping. So hiring managers have no choice but to hire job hoppers. [104] You might want to try revamping your current job before you leap into the great unknown. Otherwise, go for it.

Paid vs. Unpaid Internships

Unpaid internships usually aren't your best work bet. But they can lead to bigger and better things: needed work experience; personal contacts; a full-time, paying position with the organization you're interning for or another one you're working with who notices your excellent contributions. The bottom line is to not let an internship's lack of compensation stop you from taking the gig (if you can afford not to be paid), at least not without some research to find a way to make it pay off in future, tangible ways.

> *"Money was never a big motivation for me, except as a way to keep score. The real excitement is playing the game."* [105]

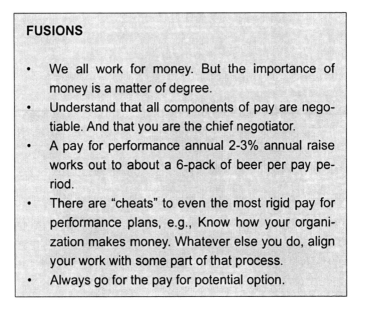

FUSIONS

- We all work for money. But the importance of money is a matter of degree.
- Understand that all components of pay are negotiable. And that you are the chief negotiator.
- A pay for performance annual 2-3% annual raise works out to about a 6-pack of beer per pay period.
- There are "cheats" to even the most rigid pay for performance plans, e.g., Know how your organization makes money. Whatever else you do, align your work with some part of that process.
- Always go for the pay for potential option.

Chapter 9
They Can't Do That!? (Can They?)
Workplace Laws and Regulations

The workplace is not a democracy, as one of our bosses said once. There are rules and regulations in the workplace that you must abide by or you'll pass Go without collecting $200.

Most of them combine pomposity with legalese, which makes for a deadly combination. Nonetheless, **there is usually a seed of something you need to know hidden deep within the verbiage**. If you can't uncover it, it'll eat you alive just like Audrey II relished her unsuspecting victims in *A Little Shop of Horrors.*

Employment law keeps many thousands of lawyers employed themselves. It is a morass of federal, state and local regulation. You have to know enough to keep your job and protect your rights. Here's a summary version.

Employee Handbook

Most of what you need to know is in your trusty Code of Corporate Conduct, a/k/a the Employee Handbook, which can run a hundred single-spaced pages in a big company. You'll have to sign a form that you've read and understood this puppy on your first day of work. Some companies have uploaded their entire handbook online, which they think makes it easier to digest. A very few companies, such as Sun Microsystems, have created interactive online game content, where you can create an avatar and role play various corporate scenarios. However the corporate Bible/Qur'an/Torah is presented in your on-boarding process, pay attention: To play the game you have to at least skim the table of contents and zero in on the essentials. Here are the cheats – the parts of the hand-book/code that you've absolutely got to get:

At Will Employment

The right of employers to fire employees for any reason, or for no reason at all, at any time. It also gives employees the legal right to quit their jobs at any time for any reason. Even so, employers may not fire employees in a way that discriminates, violates public policy or conflicts with written or implied promises they make concerning the length of employment or grounds for termination. Almost all employees are at-will employees.

Translation: If your employer decides to let you go, that's the end of your job – and you have very limited legal rights to fight it.

Equal Opportunity Employment

All employment decisions – hiring, promotion, transfer, compensation, benefits, discipline, termination – have to be made without regard to race, color, religion, sex, sexual orientation, gender identity, age, disability, national origin, citizenship/ immigration status, veteran status or any other protected status.

Translation: No one can be discriminated against in the workplace, compliments of federal law.

Sexual and Other Unlawful Harassment

Heads up on this one. Unwelcome sexual advances, requests for sexual favors, and other verbal or physical conduct of a sexual nature constitutes sexual harassment when submitting to or rejecting it does or might affect someone's employment, unreasonably interferes with someone's work performance or creates an intimidating, hostile or offensive work environment.

Translation: If your mother would yell at you for the behavior, or if you *think it might* be offensive, it probably is. Don't do it on the job, especially if your testosterone or estrogen is clouding your thinking....

Check it out:

The Top 20 Sexual-Harassment Cases of All Time

http://www.hrworld.com/features/top-20-sexual-harassment-cases-121307

Standards of Conduct

A list of guidelines regarding ethical and legal standards that all employees are expected to follow on the job; if you don't, you can be disciplined or fired. They can also apply when you're not even at work but are engaging in illegal or morally questionable acts. For example, employers do not find drug use, drunkenness or public sex acceptable on or off the job.

Translation: You are what you do. And, when you're in public, all behavior is public. Picture your boss watching you hurl on YouTube. Not a pretty picture in so many ways....

Workplace Searches

"To protect the property and ensure the safety of all employees ...the company reserves the right to conduct personal searches consistent with state law ... and to inspect any possessions carried to and from the company's property.... Because searches may result in the discovery of personal possessions or documents, employees should refrain from bringing to or creating in the workplace any item or personal property they do not wish to reveal...."

Translation: Your personal and work property can be searched at any time, for no reason. Don't bring contraband to work and don't create unauthorized material while you're at work.

Personnel File

Do you remember in junior high school when every bit of bad behavior was answered by, *"That will go on your permanent record!"?* Workplaces have permanent records, too. They're called personnel files. They typically include your employment application, a family emergency contact form, documented disciplinary action history, a resume, employee handbook and at-will employer sign off sheets, current personal information, and job references. In most states, employees can view their files when they ask to in writing – with a supervisor present. For privacy reasons, your payroll information and medical information are NOT included. For the same reason, prospective employers cannot see or be told any information in your file, including performance reviews. *To get around this stricture, many organizations are now asking prospective employees to bring a copy of their latest performance review to job interviews.*

Translation: Everything you do in the workplace goes in a paper file and follows you throughout your employment at each organization.

Job Classifications (Exempt vs. Nonexempt)

Whether your job is classified as exempt or nonexempt will determine whether you will get paid at least minimum wage and, more important, get paid overtime for working more than 40 hours in a week. This is determined by very complicated federal regulations regarding your job duties and salary, and whether you are a bona fide executive, administrative, professional, computer or outside sales employee. *Job titles do not determine exempt or nonexempt status.*

Translation: Ask your Human Resources person whether your job is exempt or nonexempt. If the

government says you should be paid overtime, you
need to get paid overtime.

Pay Periods

You need to know when you'll get paid. The timing
is regulated by state and federal law. Most states require
wages for most types of workers to be paid at least twice
during each calendar month on days designated in ad-
vance as regular paydays. (Some jobs get paid only once a
month.) Employers have to post a notice with this information. Overtime wages must be paid by the next payroll
period following the period they were earned. If you're
fired, all wages, including accrued vacation, must be paid
immediately at the time you're let go.

**Translation: When you get paid is regulated by
law, not the whim of your employer. Most employees
will get paid twice a month on a regular basis. Ask
your HR person. This is handy to know as you have
your own rent and bills to pay.**

Hours of Work

Here's a sample paragraph: Company work hours are
[_____] a.m. to [_____] p.m. Monday through Friday,
with one (unpaid) hour for lunch. Non-exempt employees receive two ten-minute paid break periods for each
full workday, one at mid-morning and one at mid-af-
ternoon, and are expected to take a lunch or meal break
midway through their shift. As for **overtime,** all non-exempt employees who work more than eight hours in one

workday will receive overtime pay at the rate of 1½ times the employee's regular rate of pay for all hours worked in excess of 8 hours in one workday or 40 hours in one work week, or in any higher amounts required by law. See also Breaks & Meal Periods, Flexible Schedules, Family & Medical Leave, Full-time Employment, Holidays, Job Sharing, Night Work & Shift Work, Part-time Employment, Recordkeeping & Reporting, Sick Leave, Travel Time, Vacation, Leave and Weekend Work.

Translation: Know what's expected in terms of daily hours. If you're told to be at work at 8:45 and to leave at 5:15, *if you can't negotiate flextime,* be there preferably before 8:45 and don't leave until at least 5:15. Start and end times are not moveable feasts without buy-in from your manager, no matter how unnecessary they appear to you. Also know the larger work time issues – vacation, holidays and sick leave, etc. These are benefits to be earned or negotiated – and they can be worth more to you than salary.

> *"For many American workers today, time's a wastin' - literally. The average worker admits to frittering away 2.09 hours per 8-hour workday, not including lunch and scheduled break-time."* [106]

Performance Reviews

Remember feeling queasy when report cards came out? You still can! All workers get employee performance reviews, where your job performance is evaluated by your manager or boss. Reviews often determine raises, promotions, new opportunities and sometimes whether you keep your job. Just like in school, meeting your job requirements just means you're adequate – nothing more. To get a better review and the goodies that go with it, figure out how to do more to enhance your overall performance and your organization's goals. Make sure your manager knows your work product, and keep a portfolio of it, along with any positive comments from colleagues, clients or customers.

Translation: You're still getting graded. But now grades = more money, better benefits (such as more vacation and stock options), better assignments. It is up to you to manage your performance and review – show your work to your advantage and do not be passive.

> We proudly present
> The soon to be relatively famous
>
> HOOTERS®
> Employee Handbook
>
> *"Only approved Orange Hooters Girl Shorts are to be worn, sized to fit, and should NOT BE SO TIGHT THAT THE BUTTOCKS SHOW."*
>
> HOOTERS®
> A fun place to work! [107]

Personal Appearance
a/k/a Workplace Dress Code and Grooming

What you look like matters. Employers can limit employees' personal expression on the job – as in clothing, grooming and body art choices – as long as they do not impinge on your civil liberties. Your employer will have a dress and grooming code in the Handbook. Here's the bottom line: *"From the employer's point of view, if you haven't mastered the simple art of presenting yourself appropriately, you probably haven't mastered the more important, complicated skills required in the workplace."*[108] Your employer can mandate uniforms, hair length, jewelry and more. Some of this may be for safety's sake, but most is in aid of the business of running a business that attracts paying clients.

We suggest being clean and not wearing perfume, and understanding that different regions have different dress codes. Men still wear suits to the office in Chicago, but rarely to the office anywhere in California. The advice from *Glamour* Magazine's fashion editor and other fashion mavens is basic: Dress for the job you want, not the one you have; dress the way your boss does; wear clothes that look good on you. Some things that dress codes routinely ban include tank tops, halter tops, or muscle shirts, clothing with foul language or obscene images, torn clothing, sweat pants or sweat suits, flip flops and hats. Lack of proper undergarments is taboo.

Be aware that jobs involving face-to-face client contact will almost always require a more professional look, no matter how casual Fridays are. Also note that prejudice still exists within corporate America about tattoos and piercings. So cover up the tats or pay the consequences. For a guide to appropriate dress, see Donald Burleson's hilarious illustrated Professional Dress Code. [109]

Translation: Like it or not, we are all immediately judged by our appearance. Employers can dictate your clothing and grooming.

Telephone, Voice Mail & Electronic Mail

Keep personal use to a minimum. Generally speaking, if your employer gives you notice —in the Handbook, for example – that you have no reasonable expectation of privacy, you don't. Your phone calls, emails and voice-mails can be monitored and are usually archived. We can't overstress this – *do not say or write anything in the workplace setting that can come back to bite you.* Because it will. This brings up another important point: **How** you say things, especially electronically, is as important as what you say. Humans are visual. Human brains are built to decode visual cues as they take in left brain information. Absent those visual cues, the receiver's personality will supply the emotional context – paranoid, aggressive, etc. So reread your emails and consider your specific recipient before you hit send. Think about your tone of voice in phone calls and voice messages. If you would not like to receive the message, don't send it. And, if possible, face-to-face communication is almost always best.

Translation: You have no right to private communication in the workplace. Practice restraint in your communications.

Postage, Shipping, Copying & Office Supplies

They are <u>not</u> yours for personal use, even if there's a warehouse full of supplies, a room full of high-end color copiers, an unsecured postage meter and a toll-free number for FedEx. These are corporate assets, and fall under somebody's budget and audit. If you take or partake without authorization, it's stealing. You will be disciplined or fired, and your entire character will come into question. Why risk it for a few bucks of free stuff?

Translation: Buy your own office supplies and stamps.

Employment Benefits, Benefits Eligibility, Medical Insurance, 401k, Stock Options, Employee Discounts, Tuition Reimbursement, Workers' Compensation

These are all important to you because they equate to money in your pocket now and in the future. And, as we've said before, some benefits are worth more than salary and raises because they give you a hook into the future, more time, peace of mind, etc.

Translation: Snuggle up with the Employee Benefits Handbook and get to know your benefits.

Immigration Status

Federal law requires that all employers complete and retain an Employment Eligibility Verification Form (I-9) for each person they hire for employment in the United States. This includes citizens and noncitizens. [110]

Translation: There's no getting around this requirement. Employers face big fines if they do not comply.

Computer Software Licensing

Unauthorized duplication of computer software is a federal offense, punishable by up to a $250,000 fine and up to five years in jail. [111] Enterprise software and shareware is anathema to organizations, as it can corrupt authorized software and foul up networks, platforms and servers, to say nothing of reducing bandwidth to a squeak and hammering holes in security protocols and firewalls.

Translation: Don't illegally duplicate software. Don't download ANY software or products without approval from your IT department.

If you want to know more workplace rules and regulations, ask your HR manager. If you want to know more than that, check out these sites:

www.EEOC.gov   The Equal Employment Opportunity Commission is a federal government agency that protects and advocates for employees' rights.

www.NLRB.gov   The National Labor Relations Board gives information on labor union and workplace rights.

www.nolo.com   Nolo is an amazing organization that prints law books. Its employee rights resource center is an excellent resource.

www.employment.findlaw.com   has an employee rights center that provides helpful information on the legal rights of workers in all phases of employment.

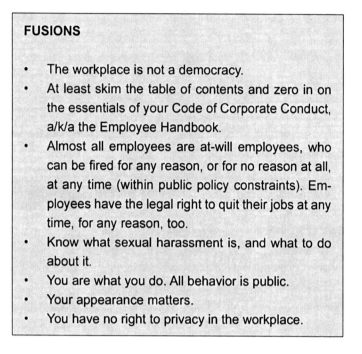

FUSIONS

- The workplace is not a democracy.
- At least skim the table of contents and zero in on the essentials of your Code of Corporate Conduct, a/k/a the Employee Handbook.
- Almost all employees are at-will employees, who can be fired for any reason, or for no reason at all, at any time (within public policy constraints). Employees have the legal right to quit their jobs at any time, for any reason, too.
- Know what sexual harassment is, and what to do about it.
- You are what you do. All behavior is public.
- Your appearance matters.
- You have no right to privacy in the workplace.

Chapter 10
Is Your 9-5 the Night of the Living Dead?
(What To Do If Your Dream Job Is a Nightmare)

> *"Believe in yourself."*
>
> The Wizard of Oz to Dorothy

Now you know what employers want, and you've landed that perfect job. So why do you want to throw up every morning before going to work?

No, it's not likely that you need a Clearblue Easy Digital Pregnancy Test, à la Juno. But you may well need some soul-searching, psyche-plumbing dialog with yourself to figure out the gap between the job you thought you got and the job you really have. In other words, stellar expectations are a classic Millennial trait, yet one of your favorite shows is *The Office*. Reality is somewhere between the two.

But **what to do with that feeling of dread**? Pay attention if you have these symptoms: [112]

You feel sick. Unhappiness at work can affect your health. If you're not partying every night, nausea, migraines, backaches, loss of libido and insomnia are signs of excess stress. Your mental health can also be damaged, as can relationships with your partner, friends and family.

You're being marginalized. Many of your responsibilities have been assigned to others, you're not included in important meetings or on email project updates. Ask your boss for the 411, but understand that this treatment is a way of asking you to leave.

People change, not to your advantage. Your favorite boss moves on, takes on a new mentee, or is himself marginalized. You no longer have access to power, plum projects or the decision-making loop. These changes may start small, but the cumulative effect on your status can be large.

You're taken for granted. Your great work gets you pegged as the new "plug 'n play" – the expert in your area. You're no longer seen as having potential for new projects, or you become known as the good corporate citizen who'll do whatever you're asked (that no one else will put up with) – redeye flights to meet clients, relocating to strange cities, working 24/7 while others get to have real lives.

You outgrow your job. You have much more experience than your job requires, but don't believe you could succeed elsewhere.

You get a better offer. You've been stuck with the same compensation for awhile, with no hope of an increase. Any other offer looks good.

Work is interfering with what's important in life. Are you falling off the teeter-totter of balancing your job and family … your job and volunteer work that gives your life meaning … your job and long-term training for a big, hairy, audacious goal? Imbalance doesn't work at work anymore than it does in the rest of life. It makes you increasingly resentful.

Boredom. You're unchallenged, need more responsibility, and want opportunities that just don't exist in your current organization. You're scattered, mildly depressed, and take forever to do simple tasks.

Anger. Anger makes you cranky and, no matter how great your work is, if you become a depressing crank, colleagues will avoid you. This isolation limits your mobility and can make you a target in a layoff or reorganization.

Your company is experiencing a downward spiral, losing customers, losing money, and rumors of possible closure, bankruptcy and failure are swirling around. Look out for number one.

Your relationship with your boss is damaged beyond repair. You've tried to fix it, but it's hopeless. If this is your fault – you've played hooky, blown by deadlines, etc., move on and don't repeat your miscreant behavior in your next job. If your boss is at fault, read The No A**hole Rule: Building a Civilized Workplace and Surviving One That Isn't by Robert I. Sutton. [113]

Your life has changed. Perhaps you've married or started a family, and the salary and benefits no longer support you. You have to accurately assess what you need to do for your family.

Your values are not in sync with the work culture. Perhaps your company has a dress code and you shop at Goodwill. Or your company has an annual holiday party and you think the money should be given to needy families. Or policy says to leave every light blazing at night to deter burglars, and you want to go minimize your carbon footprint. Whatever the clash of values, a lack of personal congruence with the corporate culture will destroy your happiness at work.

Your company is ethically challenged. Managers lie to customers about product quality and want you to fabricate the day products will ship. The company is stealing information from competitors, or cooking the books. Whatever the ethical issue, don't stay in an organization where yours are compromised.

You've developed a reputation as a slacker. That reputation is unlikely to change, so you need to carefully consider your options.

You've alienated colleagues. People have to work together well. Why-ever they don't, and your role in that dysfunction, read <u>Social Intelligence</u> by Daniel Goleman. [114]

What to do?

Do more than just suck it up. As the Nike ads say, *"Life is short. Play hard."*

First, try to fix what's wrong with your job.

Communicating with your boss is always the number-one step to take. Have the courage to have the talk. Don't be paranoid or judgmental. Just the facts ma'am is the best approach here. Lay out what you're feeling and, most important, why. Actively listen for feedback.

Don't see yourself as a wage slave. See your job as a funding source for what you want to do next. Do what's required as quickly as you can, then network like mad with those who might give you a boost to the next job.

In the interim, absorb all the training you can and try to develop new skills to take away. There's always something to learn. [115]

Take the Burnout Test [116]

To assess your stress level, complete the burnout test below, kindly made available by Dr. Arie Shirom. The Shirom-Melamed Burnout Questionnaire measures stress on the three levels that comprise the burnout condition, emotional exhaustion (EE), physical fatigue (PF), and cognitive weariness (Cog).

Answer each of the statements below by indicating how often you have the feeling during working hours. Almost always = 1 point; very frequently = 2 points; quite frequently = 3; sometimes = 4; quite infrequently = 5; very infrequently = 6; almost never = 7. Add up your scores for each of the three categories. To find your stress range, see below.

The Burnout Test

I feel tired. (PF)
I feel physically fatigued. (PF)
I feel physically exhausted. (PF)
When I get up in the morning to go to work, I have no energy. (PF)
I feel fed up. (EE)
I feel like my emotional batteries are dead. (EE)
I feel burned out in my job. (EE)
I feel emotionally fatigued. (EE)
I am too tired to think clearly. (Cog)

> I have difficulty concentrating. (Cog)
> My thinking process is slow. (Cog)
> I have difficulty thinking about complex things. (Cog)
>
> (Dr. Shirom says that men whose scores average 3.0 to 3.75 and women who average 3.6 to 4.0 are at the high end of the burnout range and should seek expert help for preventative measures.)

Leaving on Good Terms

> *"Frankly, my dear, I don't give a damn."*
>
> Rhett Butler [117]

Your grandparents probably told you not to burn your bridges. In Boomer-speak, that means don't tell people off just for the sake of telling them off. Since you're young and on a low rung of the career ladder, you'll likely need a good reference from each job for a few more years.

Here are five temptations to avoid:

1. Don't tell off your boss or co-workers, even if they deserve it.

When you leave a job, you might be PO'd, especially if you're leaving on less than optimal terms. You may want to tell people – including your boss – what you truly think of them. Don't do it, even if they truly deserve it. Six degrees of separation dictate that you'll meet up with some of them again down the career path and, especially if you stay in the same industry, you may work with them somewhere again.

2. Don't damage company property, steal something or mess with the IT systems.

Even if you feel used and abused, vandalism, theft and viruses are criminal offenses. Your professional rep can be destroyed, and you could end up serving time.

3. Don't forget to ask for a reference.

This may sound weird if you're leaving your job badly. Since the job will be on your resume anyway, you should try for a decent reference – in writing to take with you. If you've been fired for malfeasance, don't even ask, but if you're leaving for a less serious reason, ask your boss for a reference, despite the job not working out as you both would have liked.

4. Don't denigrate your organization, boss or colleagues to whoever replaces you.

Whining will get you nothing. Let your successor figure things out. You might have just had bad chemistry. Your replacement may have a great experience, even in the same circumstances.

5. Don't disparage your employer in job interviews.

No one likes a whiner. Your prospective boss will wonder what caused your previous job to go bad, and will suspect it was you.

Get a great new job. The best revenge is living well!

Drink the Kool-Aid, Just Don't Chug It.

"Bureaucracies are little subcultures that sometimes seem more like cults. Take sales meetings. They bear a cult's tell-tale signs: leader (an over-caffeinated VP of sales), mantra ("Accelerate in 2008!"), big production number ("The Future's So Bright, I Gotta Wear Shades"), and ritualistic insignia (logo-emblazoned totes). I sit in the back where nobody can catch me scrawling "KILL ME PLEASE" on my handout." [118]

FUSIONS

- Do more than just suck it up: Try to fix what's wrong with your job.
- Communicating with your boss is always the number-one step to take. Have the courage to have the talk.
- Don't see yourself as a wage slave. See your job as a funding source for what you want to do next.
- Leave on the best terms possible. Think 6 degrees of separation – you likely will work with some of these people again.
- Get a great new job. The best revenge is living well!

Onward

> *"The best way to predict the future is to create it."*
>
> Ken Allen

The nature of work is transforming across every industry sector. The keys to competitive success are now human and virtual intelligence ... creativity ... the ability to accurately assess the motivational profiles of clients, customers, colleagues and vendors ... global outlook in terms of influences, markets and resources ... just-in-time innovation and ... truly collaborative relationships. [119]

To unlock that future, **organizations need to create unique, personalized experiences in the workplace for every employee,** unleashing and leveraging the capabilities of each worker, playing off the experience and unique strengths of both generations and individuals. In other words, Boomers' experience, perseverance and social conscience; and Millennials' boundaryless perspective, technological wizardry and need for meaningful work must fuse and create the future of each organization.

A third workplace revolution is transforming our businesses from the inside out. The first traded farms for factories. The second swapped muscles for minds. The third revolution is the shift from left-brain to right-brain creative economic production, a shift brought on by the

World Wide Web and its digitization, connectivity and globalization. We believe that Boomers will be the midwives or enablers, and Millennials the producers of this shift. Their unique core competencies are a perfect fit to prime the global creative economy.

The U.S. is at the forefront of this new world. Our creative sector now accounts for more than $2 trillion USD—or nearly half—of all wages and salaries paid in the U.S. Over the next decade, it's projected to add 10 million more creative sector jobs. At the current rate of increase, the number of creative jobs will soon eclipse the number of manufacturing jobs. [120]

This has changed the rules of competition.

The true source of value creation is creative talent, especially that of the Millennials. As we said in chapter 1, *"… (T)his generation … has been shaped not by understanding the natural world and manipulating its resources, but by artificial intelligence and virtual relationships."* **Organizations that recruit and motivate their own creative workers will win.**

Resources matter. There's a reason why Google attracts the best and the brightest. The hard and soft cutting-edge technology it offers employees, plus excellent salaries and benefits and world-class colleagues, has created a culture that optimizes each employee's potential and contribution, and offers an incubator for each employee's ideas and innovations.

But accessing the creative economy is not limited to the best educated creative workers, or to emerging technologies. The creative economy is endemic.

Many organizations operating across the globe – Starbucks, Whole Foods, Target, Best Buy – are trying to enable employees to jump service work into the space of innovation and creativity. They are ramping up pay, and creating workplaces where employees can use their unique perspectives and creative talents to enrich customer experiences and generate additional revenues. Best Buy's value statements say it all: *"(To) provide opportunities for employees to bring forward new ideas, new thinking ... (for) each employee to contribute their unique ideas and experiences in service of customers ... (to) unleash the power of our people ... (to) have fun while being the best."* [121]

> "Small changes made on the salesroom floor—by a Millennial sales rep re-conceiving a Vonage display or an immigrant salesperson acting to increase outreach, advertising, and service to non-English-speaking communities—have been implemented nationwide, generating hundreds of millions of dollars in added revenue." [122]

To thrive going forward, organizations need to:

- Create workplaces that attract, retain, and motivate creative talent
- Eliminate artificial boundaries (organizational structures, generational outlooks, industry seg-

ments, geographic borders, product lines, intellectual ownership)

- Leverage technology
- Incubate creativity
- Welcome innovation
- Foster commonalities among all parties to business relationships – team members, consumers, suppliers
- Enable work to be done ubiquitously – when and where needed
- Accelerate productivity

> *"In the 21st century, brainpower and imagination, invention and the organization of new technologies are the key strategic ingredients...." [123]*

What will our organizations look like when they can do all this? [124]

They will reflect our choices: What products and services will we offer? How will we produce and sell them? What kind of workplace will we create? How will we create human capital sustainability? How will we build and strengthen relationships in every aspect of our business? What roles will we play in our social and physical environment? How will we fuse our employees' strengths to prime our future in the creative economy?

We also have choices to make as individuals: What kind of work ignites my passions? What kind of organizations will I work for? Where can I make my best contribution? How will I integrate work and life? How will I find meaning in my work? How will I make a difference in the social and community causes that are important to me?

The choices we make for our organizations and ourselves will inform and create the future. We hope that this book has given you facts, insight and curiosity about the creative economy before us, and how to get there.

""When the rate of change inside an institution becomes slower than the rate of change outside, the end is in sight. The only question is when."

Jack Welch, former CEO, General Electric

⌘   ⌘   ⌘

"It seems to go right down to the heart of human nature – what we workers get out of our jobs intrinsically, emotionally, and physically."

Matt Finkelstein www.futuresense.com/blog 05/08

At **FutureSense, our goal is to engage people to speed results,** whether we're doing organizational development, succession planning, training, compensation, strategic planning or communications work.

We are committed to change: to change the way people think about management and how organizations work, and to help business leaders affect change in their organizations.

Put simply: We will change the way you do business.

With FUSE, we've tried to put that philosophy in play by offering our ideas about how to ignite the full power of the creative economy.

We'd like to hear your thoughts and ideas about the 20th century workplace and the 21st century workforce, or anything else related.

To give us feedback, read our blog or e-zine, take our Millennials' survey, or book a speaker, contact us at:

www.futuresense.com 415-453-1514

To learn more about FUSE, go to www.futuresense.com/ FUSE

About Us

Jim Finkelstein The founder of FutureSense, Jim Finkelstein has more than 32 years of consulting and corporate experience. Throughout his career as a Partner in a Big Five firm, a CEO of a professional services firm, a corporate executive for Fortune 500 companies, and an entrepreneur, Jim developed an expertise in analyzing business models from multiple angles and transforming office cultures.

Jim studies the convergence of environment, culture, development, incentive and compensation needed to improve business performance through human capital. He has applied his competencies in all areas that impact people at work—from why they show up to why they stay.

Jim received a B.A. in Psychology and Economics from Trinity College and an M.B.A. in Organization Behavior and Development from the Wharton School of the University of Pennsylvania.

See www.futuresense.com

Mary Gavin has over 25 years' experience in executive-level communications. She has managed communications departments for Bank of America, the Bar Association of San Francisco and SPG Solar, as well as advised Fortune 500, national nonprofit, dot.com, and state and federal government organizations on communications strategies, content, and crisis management. Mary is especially interested in converging information steams and transcending words with graphics-rich, interactive content using media 2.0 technologies – 3-D website portals, webinars, blogs, podcasts, videos – to engage and captivate audiences.

Mary received her J.D. from the School of Law at the University of California, Davis, where she was Executive Editor of the Law Review. She earned her B.A. in Political Theory from The George Washington University, Washington, D.C.

See www.gavinmedia.org

Notes on Sources

Starting Point

1 Daniel Pink, <u>A Whole New Mind: Why Right-Brainers Will Rule the Future</u> (New York: Penguin Group USA 2005) 1

2 http://www.akkamsrazor.com/tag/psychology

3 See Wm. Strauss & Neil Howe, <u>Generations</u> (New York: William Morrow 1991) and Neil Howe & Wm. Strauss, <u>Millennials Rising</u> (New York: Vintage Books 2000); John Beck & Mitchell Wade, <u>Got Game</u> (Boston: Harvard Business School Publishing 2004); Ben Rigby, <u>Mobilizing Generation 2.0</u> (San Francisco: John Wiley & Sons 2008), Jean Twenge, <u>Generation Me</u> (New York: Free Press 2006); http://www.marcprensky.com; http://www.mccrindle.com.au; http://blog.penelopetrunk.com

For Employers

4 Dr. Michael Kannisto, *Three Questions to Ask Yourself About Millennials*, 12/28/07 www.ere.net

5 The Millennials: Bureau of Labor Statistics, 2003 www.bls.gov as quoted in http://www.nasrecruitment.com/talenttips/NASinsights/GenerationY.pdf p. 8

6 Nancy Aldrich, *Finders-Keepers Strategies*, July/August 2001 p. 17 http://www.lib.niu.edu/2001/ip010715.html

Chapter 1

7 Nadira Hira, *Attracting the Twentysomething Worker*, Fortune Magazine 05/15/07

8 There are many different ways to define Millennials. The way that makes the most sense to us is to include the 80 million Americans roughly between the ages of 15 and 30, born largely between 1980 and 1995.

9 John Naisbitt, <u>Megatrends</u> (Australia: Warner Books 1982) 10

10 Entitlement Generation 12/05; http://www.fsu.com/pages/2005/09/29/workplace_tensions.html http://www.quarterlifecrisis.biz/qc_stats.htm,; Linda Gravett and Robin Throckmorton, <u>Bridging the Generation</u> Gap (New Jersey: Career Press 2007) 21

11 John Beck & Mitchell Wade, <u>Got Game: How the Gamer Generation is Reshaping Business Forever</u> (Boston: Harvard Business School Publishing 2004); Jean Twenge, <u>Generation Me</u> (New York: Free Press 2006)

12 Beck, 37

13 Beck, 1-26

14 Russ Eckel, *Learning Along with the Millennials* http://downloads.generationsatwork.net/training.pdf.

15 Beck, 90

16 http://humanresources.about.com/od/management-tips/a/millennial_myth_2.htmMyths About Millennials

Chapter 2

17 Headline of satirical article theonion.com 04252008; mccrindle.com.au/wp_pdf/NewGenerationsAtWork.pdf,

18 http://www.exclusiveconcepts.com/50.html

19 Ryan Healy, *3 More New Marketing Rules for Recruiting Millennials*, 2/14/08 http://www.employeeevolution.com/archives/2008/02

20 *A Grad at the Launching Pad ... Hoping Dad Won't Get Mad!* Eric Chester Whys News Issue #57 May 2006 http://www.generationwhy.com/blog/

21 http://www.mccrindle.com.au/wp_pdf/NewGenerationsAtWork.pdf

22 Marc Prensky, *Digital Natives Digital Immigrants* (2001)

23 http://www.mccrindle.com.au/wp_pdf/Seriously-Cool.pdf

24 *Generation Y: The Millennials Ready or Not, Here They Come,* http://www.nasrecruitment.com/ TalentTips/NASinsights/GenerationY.pdf

25 http://www.retailcustomerexperience.com/article.php?id=391&prc=32&page=43

26 Carolyn Martin and Bruce Tulgan, <u>Managing the Generation Mix: From Collision to Collaboration</u> (Amherst: HRD Press 2002); http://www.mccrindle.com.au/wp_pdf/NewGenerationsAtWork.pdf; http://www.retailcustomerexperience.com/article.php?id=391

27 http://www.hrworld.com/features/10-online-recruiting-blogs-040308

28 www.LinkedIn.com

29 phttp://www.cpa2biz.com/Content/media/PRO-DUCER_CONTENT/Newsletters/Articles_2008/CorpFin/Y.js

30 Robin Allen, *Managers Must Set Example for Gen Y Kid-ployees;* 2005 nasrecruitment.com/talenttips/NASin-sights/GenerationY.pdf; Jonas Ridderstrale and Kjell Nordstrom, <u>Funky Business: Talent Makes Capital Dance</u> (London: English Times Management 2002)

Chapter 3

31 http://jscms.jrn.columbia.edu/cns/2005-12-27/re-imer-officelingo, http://www.techyness.com/?cat=27

32 Nicholas Carr, *What the Internet Is Doing To Our Brains*, Atlantic Magazine, cover, "Is Google Making Us Stoopid?" July/August 2008

33 McCrindle Research, *Word Up*, 2008 http://www.mc-crindle.com.au/wp_pdf/Wordup_Lexicon.pdf

34 http://www.generationwhy.com

35 McCrindle Research, *Word Up*, 2008 http://www.mc-crindle.com.au/wp_pdf/Wordup_Lexicon.pdf

36 http://www.hotel-online.com/Trends/CarolVerret/GenerationY_Nov2000.html

37 Andrew Tilin, *How to Speak Millennial: Lessons From a B-School Dean* http://www.bnet.com/2403-13059_23-201746.html

38 www.blogtalkradio.com/Y-Talk

39 www.buzzwhack.com

40 *Hunh? What Makes You Think They Are Reading Your Stuff?* http://www.jackconsultingllc.com/index.php/discussion/9

Chapter 4

41 HR Magazine May 2007; Fortune Magazine 5/28/07

42 http://www.tmtd.biz/category/millennial-generation

43 Ryan Healy, *10 Ways Generation Y Will Change the Workplace* http://www.employeeevolution.com/archives/2008/05/23/10-ways-generation-y-will-change-the-workplace

44 Marc Prensky, *Capturing the Value of "Generation Tech" Employees* http://www.strategy-business.com/en-ewsarticle/enews063004?pg=all

45 http://www.generationwhy.com

46 http://www.wisdompage.com/LernerReview.html

47 Marc Prensky, *Digital Natives Digital Immigrants* 2001; *The Emerging Online Life Of The Digital Native* 2004

48 http://www.strategy-business.com/press/enewsarticle/enews063004?pg=0

49 http://innovationfeeder.files.wordpress.com/ 2007/08/gen-x-y-in-oz-workforce.doc

50 http://hbswk.hbs.edu/item/5736.html

51 http://www.keepingthepeople.com/_articles/IEETA-AFG.pdf

52 http://employeeevolution.com

53 http://www.gentrends.com/getting_Millennials_to_engage.html

54 thinkinghttp://www.mccrindle.com.au/wp_pdf/SeriouslyCool.pdf

55 McCrindle Research, *The ABC of XYZ* 2008 http://www.mccrindle.com.au

56 http://www.beyond.com/Media/Generation-Y-In-The-Workplace.asp; www.BrazenCareerist.com 05/23/08

57 Ryan Healy, *Crystal Ball: 10 Ways Generation Y Will Change the Workplace*, www.brazencareerist.com 5/23/08

58 William Gibson

Chapter 5

59 http://www.mobilize.org/index.php?tray=content&tid=top364&cid=11DS10

60 http://www.collegescholarships.org/loans/average-debt.htm

61 http://www.mobilize.org/index.php?tray=content&tid=top364&cid=11DS10

62 *2007 Job Satisfaction: A Survey Report by the Society for Human Resource Management*

63 http://www.mobilize.org/index.php?tray=content&tid=top364&cid=11DS10

64 http://www.universumglobal.com/CMSTemplates/Universum.com/files/USpressrelease/UndergradTrendRelease.pdf 2007http://blog.penelopetrunk.com/2007/05/31/new-financial-data-highlights-generational-rifts

65 http://www.talentmgt.com/compensation_benefits/2008/February/542/index.php?pt=a&aid=542&start=3088&page=2

66 http://www.talentmgt.com/performance_manage-
   ment/2008/January/526/index.php?pt=a&aid=526
   &start=6770&page=3http://www.talentmgt.com/
   compensation_benefits/2007/February/239/index.
   php?pt=a&aid=239&start=3415&page=2

67 http://knowledge.emory.edu/article.
   cfm?articleid=950

68 http://www.talentmgt.com/compensation_bene-
   fits/2007/February/239/index.php?pt=a&aid=239&s
   tart=3415&page=2

69 http://www.hotjobsresources.com/pdfs/Millennial-
   Workers.pdf

70 http://www.annaliotta.typepad.com

Bridge
71 Ryan Healy http://blog.penelopetrunk.com/2007/04/
   25/twentysomething-paychecks-are-boring

For Millennials
72 Marc Prensky, *The Emerging Online Life of the Digital Native* 2004

73 http://blog.penelopetrunk.com/2008/07/11/how-to-
   figure-out-how-much-you-should-be-paid/ 07/11/08

74 *San Francisco Chronicle* 6/15/06

75 Walter Raleigh, Sr. (1554?-1618)

Chapter 6
76 http://www.jobopeningsblog.com/jobs/2006/09/
   what_do_employe.html

77 http://www.google.com/corporate/culture.html

78 http://www.employmenttimesonline.com/career_advisor/article.php?ID=658

79 http://www.quintcareers.com/job_skills_values.html

80 http://www.itheadhunter.ca/careerresourcecanada/articlesfull/2.shtml

81 http://www.damngood.com/jobseekers/tipsToo.html

82 Tom Peters, *100 Ways to Succeed #120* http://www.tompeters.com/entries.php?note=010426.php 06/02/08

83 See www.vault.com/surveys/social-networking/index.jsp and www.abilitiesenhanced.com/digital-dirt.pdf

84 http://www.privacyrights.org/fs/fs16-bck.htm#2

85 http://www.funpike.com/view/Jokes/At-Work/The-Perfect-Employee

Chapter 7

86 http://psychologytoday.com/articles/pto-19940701-000025.html http://johnplaceonline.com/be-successful/the-9-factors-of-workplace-happiness

87 Daniel Goleman, <u>Emotional Intelligence: Why It Can Matter More Than IQ</u> (New York: Bantam 1997)

88 http://research.lawyers.com/Research-Reveals-Rise-in-Interoffice-Romance.html

89 http://humanresources.about.com/cs/workrelationships/a/workromance.htm

90 Thomas Edison; Sam Ewing

91 http://blog.penelopetrunk.com/2008/05/13/why-you-should-never-complain-about-your-company

92 http://blog.guykawasaki.com/2007/05/the_nine_ bigges.html

93 http://192.220.96.182/joke_3lies.html

94 http://www.allbusiness.com/finance/3592324-1.

95 http://www.boundless.org/2005/articles/a0001195. cfm

96 http://www.management-issues.com/2007/5/8/ research/boomer-or-slacker-were-all-the-same.asp

97 Terry Pratchett, <u>Moving Pictures</u> (UK: Victor Gollancz Ltd. 2002)

Chapter 8

98 *Don't Wait for Retirement to Live the Good Life. Do it Now* http://blog.penelopetrunk.com/3/20/08

99 http://www.entrepreneur.com/humanresources/man-agingemployees/article179200.html

100 © FutureSense, Inc. 2008

101 *Employer Perceptions About Job Satisfaction Factors Are Not Employee Reality* 01/06 http://www.salary.com/abou-tus/layoutscripts/abtl_default.asp?tab=abt&cat= cat012&ser=ser041&part=Par496

102 Shari Caudron, *Master the Compensation Maze* 1993 http://www.workforce.com/archive/feature/ 22/18/22/index.php

103 http://www.shrm.org/diversity/library_published/ nonIC/CMS_019637.asp

104 http://hotjobs.yahoo.com/career-articles-will_job_ hopping_hurt_your_career-339

105 Donald Trump (1946 -) <u>Trump: Art of the Deal</u>

Chapter 9

106 http://www.salary.com/careers/layouthtmls/crel_display_nocat_Ser374_Par555.html

107 http://www.thesmokinggun.com/archive/0915051hooters1.html

108 http://www.appleone.com/Career_Seekers/ToolsAndResources/Core/core_17.aspx

109 http://www.dba-oracle.com/dress_code.htm

110 http://www.uscis.gov/portal/site/uscis/menuitem.5af9bb95919f35e66f614176543f6d1a/

111 Better Business Bureau, *Computer Software Piracy* 03/25/03 http://us.bbb.org/WWWRoot/SitePage.aspx?site=113&id=1869d6a9-82aa-49a1-8419-40a8251fa916&art=406

Chapter 10

112 http://careerplanning.about.com/od/quittingyourjob/a/when_to_quit.htm; http://humanresources.about.com/od/whenemploymentends/a/quit_job_3.htm

113 Robert Sutton, <u>The No A**hole Rule: Building a Civilized Workplace and Surviving One That Isn't</u> (New York: Hachette Book Group USA 2007)

114 Daniel Goleman, <u>Social Intelligence: The New Science of Human Relationships</u> (New York: Bantam 2006)

115 http://money.cnn.com/2005/07/26/commentary/everyday/sahadi/ind ex.htm?cnn=yes

116 http://www.worktolive.info/poen_burn.cfm

117 Rhett Butler, Gone with the Wind

118 Anne Altman, "Tips From a Bitter Temp" *Business Week* 8/25/08 p. 59

Onward

119 We are informed here by many works that envision innovation and future thinking, including C.K. Prahalad and M.S. Krishnan, <u>The New Age of Innovation: Driving Co-created Value through Global Networks</u> (New York: McGraw Hill 2008) Clayton Christensen, <u>The Innovator's Dilemma: When New Technologies Cause Great Firms to Fail</u> (Boston: Harvard Business School Press 1997), Clayton Christensen and Michael Raynor, <u>The Innovator's Solution: Creating and Sustaining Successful Growth</u> (Boston: Harvard Business School Press 2003)

120 Richard Florida, *"A Search for Jobs in Some of the Wrong Places", USA Today* 02/12/06 http://www.usatoday.com/news/opinion/editorials/2006-02-12-bush-jobs_x.htm

121 http://www.bestbuyinc.com/corporate_responsibility, *Best Buy Fiscal 2008 Corporate Responsibility Report* May 2008

122 http://www.cato-unbound.org/2006/06/04/richard-florida/the-future-of-the-american-workforce-in-the-global-creative-economy

123 Lester Thurow, Economist

124 Robert J. Laubacher, Thomas W. Malone, and the MIT Scenario Working Group, *Two Scenarios for 21st Century Organizations: Shifting Networks of Small Firms or All-Encompassing "Virtual Countries"* 1997 http://ccs.mit.edu/21c/21cwpmain.html

Made in the USA